"This book is the most thorough and complete treatise on the art and craft of directing film for the newcomer who wants to learn directing. It's written in a style that is understandable and interesting which brings clear truth and insights to the reader."

    – Donn Cambern, editor of *Easy Rider*

Praise for William Dickerson's film *Detour:*

"Think of the blackest crawl space you encountered as a child, and then imagine curling up inside it, at midnight, for the better part of 90 minutes, and you're getting close to the experience of watching writer/director William Dickerson's debut feature, *Detour*—and, yes, that's a compliment."

    – *The Village Voice*

"This taut and effective thriller produces maximum suspense with a minimum of means."

    – *The Hollywood Reporter*

"*Detour* is the best US film I've seen in 2013."

    – Tom Charity

"Dicker...
techni... any
amoul...
Detou...

    – *P...*

"It take... ide
witho...

    – *T...*

"At times the groan and scream of collapsing metal sounds so authentic you might mistake Jackson's heavy breathing for your own."

– *The New York Times*

"A claustrophobic nail-biter!"

– Film Pulse

"Dickerson's set-ups and sense of drama in *Detour* is really on key. I think he did a better job of directing this than Danny Boyle of *127 Hours*."

– Henry Sheehan, KPCC's "Film Week"

"I had gotten to know this character so well that I was rooting for him to be able to somehow get himself out of this predicament and back home to his life. And if I found myself rooting for that, I think *Detour* was a success."

– Ain't It Cool News

"Dickerson's creative use of angles and small camera movements serve to enhance the swelling anxiety of his economical screenplay while constantly keeping us on edge."

– *TV Guide*

"Ultimately you are drawn into the dire circumstances and forget how the camera covers them as the poor protagonist gulps for air under tons of dirt. For every breath he's grasping for, you're holding one in, anticipating what might follow."

– *Film Threat*

"I can't help but relate this film to others like *127 Hours* or *Buried*, since it deals with the same issues of being isolation in a confined space and the struggle to survive. Those were good films but I have to say I was absolutely blown away with *Detour*. I will be spreading the word like a wildfire since this is a film that people need to see."

– Media Mikes

HOLLYWOOD

How
To
Direct
a
Microbudget
Film

(or any film, for that matter)

WILLIAM DICKERSON

Book Layout: Gina Mansfield
Editor: Jane Gould

Kettle of Letters Press
Los Angeles, CA

ISBN: 978-0-9851886-3-4
Library of Congress Control Number: 2014918213

CONTENTS

ACKNOWLEDGMENTS

This book would not have been possible without the unwavering support of my teachers and mentors over my many years pursuing the art and craft of filmmaking:

Jane Burke, Father Brennan, S.J., Father O'Malley, S.J., Steve Vineberg, Edward Isser, Jack O'Connell, Robert Cording, Peter Markham, Rob Spera, Jim McBride, D.C. Fontana, Donn Cambern, Robert Mandel and George Walczak.

I can't thank you enough.

Thanks to my friends, colleagues and family, especially my parents, Patricia and Thomas Dickerson, my sister, Briana, and my loving wife, Rachel. I also want to thank my editor, Jane Gould, and layout designer, Gina Mansfield, for doing amazing work on this book, and B. J. Markel for helping me put all the pieces of this publishing puzzle together.

Finally, a special thanks to everyone involved in the making of *Detour*. Each and every one of you made the impossible possible.

microbudget film, n. :
1. a movie made for less than one million dollars, but often for much less than that, and with no help from Hollywood.

INTRODUCTION

If you're reading this, you probably haven't made a feature film—at least not one with a budget of substantial measure starring bankable actors—and haven't sold a screenplay to a company that's a signatory of the Writer's Guild of America. If this is true, perfect. You're exactly the person who should be reading this. If you happen to be one of *those persons* ("those persons" being defined as persons who actually make a living writing or directing in this business of movies), I still suggest you keep reading. You're making some money now; it's nice to support your fellow artist.

I am a filmmaker who has written and directed shorts and features that have played in festivals around the country, won awards and have been watched, evaluated and critiqued by Academy-Award winners. I helped spearhead the first film program in the history of my undergraduate school, The College of The Holy Cross in Worcester, Massachusetts. I received a Master of Fine Arts Degree in Directing from the American Film Institute Conservatory (AFI), which consistently ranks among the top three film schools in the world by *The Hollywood Reporter*. I have served on the Admissions Committee for AFI and am currently on the Executive Board for the school's Alumni Mentorship Program. I also teach Director's Craft courses at the New York Film Academy in Los Angeles. My debut feature film *Detour* was acquired by Level 1 Entertainment and released theatrically and On Demand through Gravitas Ventures and Warner Brothers Digital Distribution. The film has been described as "the best U.S. film I've seen in 2013" by Tom Charity, an "emotional and psychological roll-er-coaster ride" by *The Examiner*, and nothing short of "authentic" by *The New York Times*. I've been hired to direct commercials, documentaries and music videos. Several of my feature-length screenplays have been optioned or have been in development at major production companies. I've also been paid to rewrite other people's scripts.

Finally, the least impressive credential, but perhaps most important, is that I currently live in Hollywood, California.

I'm not originally from Los Angeles. When people ask me how I like Los Angeles, I respond succinctly that the thought never really crossed my mind. It's an irrelevant question, as it's a mere circumstance. I liken Los Angeles to a war zone—a *battleground*, if you will—that I have airdropped myself into as part of a classified mission to complete a target objective. My father was a Special Forces Green Beret, who did his fair share of paratrooping in Vietnam; therefore, this feels like an appropriate analogy.

Or perhaps it is a desperate attempt to wheedle my father into understanding what I'm trying to do out here, which is undertaking a profession he has been trying to convince me not to pursue for years.

I didn't move to Los Angeles to enjoy the land. Unless you're a lover of concrete and questionable air quality, Hollywood is largely unappealing on a spiritual level. The church I frequent is the church of movies, and that church is located in this town. Its parishioners wander the streets, live in the bungalows adjacent to me, and wait in long lines with me at the Post Office to mail their scripts to the next agent on their lists. This place is, without question, the metropolis of dreams.

Nevertheless, the flipside of the dream is the nightmare, and as bright as the sun shines out here, it goes down at night, and it can get real dark out in the LA desert.

My story is chock full of advice, of important tips and tutorials, and also of fundamental caution for the aspiring filmmaker. I will share with you an abundance of film school insight, which I'm still paying off, and will illustrate this insight with examples from the real world of making movies. I will share with you the gritty details of how I made my first feature film *Detour*. I hope to, at best, inspire and, at the very least, entertain.

There is a stockpile of books already on the shelves about how to write a screenplay, or how to direct a film, and many are filled with invaluable experiences from some of the most seasoned veterans of film, television and theatre. Many of these books I highly recommend and urge you to add to your own growing collection. The lessons that I offer in these pages are from my own firsthand experience, experience that has been influenced by an amalgamation of classroom lessons, books I've read on the subject, and functional knowledge. You need to do more than merely absorb; you need to go out there and implement the rules and skills you've learned in a real environment. I've done that and it helped me not only complete my first feature, but also see that feature projected onto the big screen at Mann's Chinese Theatre.

Part instructional, part anecdotal, this book will shed light on the world of directing, and the world in which directing takes place. Hopefully, seeing how I apply the rules I've learned to practical situations will be valuable to you and motivate you to either follow in this same path or map out an entirely new one. I will share with you a blueprint of my approach to the craft; it's the same approach I take on each of my films, and the approach works.

The movie industry is a race to stay fresh. It's a struggle to stay relevant, and relevancy in this business is what pays the bills. I will teach you how to direct a microbudget film, or a film of any budget for that matter, and I will use *Detour* as an example of how I made a movie, sold the movie, and got the movie distributed worldwide.

THE DIRECTOR'S CHAIR

WHAT IS A DIRECTOR?

The answer is quite simple: a director is a storyteller.

A story is a narrative, either true or fictitious, that is designed to interest, amuse or instruct the viewer, that is about something. The *telling* part is the method through which the story is told (in our case, filmmaking).

This book should serve as a practical and compact guide for film-makers, both beginners and professionals alike, on "how-to" direct. It's a book to underline, dog-ear pages and pull out on set when in a bind. It's also a book to reflect on when considering how to make your movie in the current state of the business. Before I get into the behind-the-scenes of *Detour*, I'd like to share the essentials. In other words, this is what a director really needs to know.

THE DIRECTOR AS THE SOLE DEFENSE FOR THE STORY

The buck stops with the producer, but the idea falls under the authority of the director. However, any director worth his or her peers' respect is apt to encourage as many ideas as possible from the heads of the creative departments. It doesn't matter how many hours, days, weeks, months, or years you've spent prepping your film, you will not have thought of everything.

I spent the better part of three years prepping my film *Detour* and I didn't come close to thinking of everything that could facilitate the telling of its story. However, it's important to remember that every person involved with the project, no matter what his or her specific job is, is there to make the same film you are, and they can help.

Ideally, the smartest decision that you can make is to suspend your ego and surround yourself with people who are all smarter than you. The most important job a director has, aside from casting the film properly, is encouraging ideas, being able to recognize when the ideas are good, and then incorporating these good ideas into the film.

While you do want to explore these ideas, it is also important to convey, in as polite a manner as possible, that it is the director's job to determine which ideas work to advance the story, and which do not. Furthermore, if you decide that an idea does not work, the conjurer of said idea must respect that decision. **An effective way to help everyone understand this concept is to stress the fact that the director is the *sole defense for the story*.**

Remind your eager collaborators that when the film comes out, if it fails, it is the director who will undoubtedly be blamed for its failure—not the production designer, not the cinematographer, not the actors, not even the screenwriter, but the director. In a business where reputation is literally everything, it is the director's reputation that is on the line. It often helps to communicate these stakes to the cast, crew and others who feel their opinions must be validated.

These stakes are what make the director the only unbiased artist involved in the production. As a director, you're not fighting for the integrity of a particular department. Rather, you're worrying about the story as it is represented as a whole. If the story fails, you fail—and this contingency demands respect.

"Directing Is the Omnipotence of Impotence"

The above phrase was something that a college professor of mine, Ed Isser, used in his theatre directing class. It really stuck with me. What he meant by it, exactly, is that directing is an attempt to control chaos, to catch lightning in a bottle, *per se*. You may be under the impression that you have the narrative worked out, every frame of the film storyboarded, every beat outlined, and every possible adjustment for the actor formulated ahead of time. But, the generator will break down, and suddenly you can't shoot indoors anymore. Or, the arrangement of the furniture and the positioning of the actors between this furniture—which you needed to externalize the characters' willful ignorance of their failing marriage as they lose themselves within a labyrinth of mice-like daily routine—is impossible on a set that looks like a vacant lot lacking the most simple of outdoor lounge chairs!

Everything that can go wrong, will go wrong.

I suggest that you embrace this one simple truth; it is so ordained by the movie gods. Prepare as much as you possibly can, but also be prepared to throw everything away at a moment's notice if the circumstances are altered. Once you determine what the scene is about, this knowledge will guide you through these unforeseen obstacles and allow you to say the same thing, just framed, lit or colored a slightly different way. The ability to improvise is lost if one is only prepared to communicate the idea through only one approach.

MAKING DIRECTING TANGIBLE

I don't want to bore you with too much of the academics involved in directing. To do so would be tedious and potentially violate the mystique of the art form—though I actually had a professor who taught a class on mystique, and there were some meat and potatoes to what he had to say. I often joke that the directing program is the hardest program to get into at the American Film Institute, my alma mater, because everyone wants to direct, but it's also the one program in which you graduate with no tangible skills. Editors create timelines in Avid or Final Cut Pro, cinematographers hold cameras and point them at things, writers print out paper with words on them, production designers actually build stuff, but directors? What do directors do?

On the surface, directing doesn't seem to require any tangible skills. That's the reason why everyone in the business thinks they can direct. At the same time, most would never dare try. They are horrified at the thought of talking to actors, for one, in addition to communicating a concrete creative vision to every department in the production. On one hand, you have an idea, a script, usually based on some kind of intellectual conceit, some kind of high concept. It is completely left brain. And on the other, you have the actors, the conduits to the emotion of the story, who are zeniths of raw emotions themselves. It is completely right brain. The director is the bridge between both of the sides.

The real point is if a film is good it's like experiencing magic, and the director who conjured that black magic will be hired again to conjure up some more. It's as straightforward as that. It's that uncomplicated. But if the film sucks, the director won't be working again anytime soon.

This means that if you want to be a director, you can't just go and get a job out of school with the kind of ease your classmates in the other disciplines at film school can. For the first couple of years after graduation, you may find yourself at home, in your pajamas, at your computer writing and on the phone begging, borrowing and stealing whatever morsel of currency you can get your hands on. This is because there's only one option for you: the director needs to go and direct a film, by hook or by crook. Even if it's completely DIY, in doing it yourself, you will prove you're a leader, a go-getter, a manager as well as an artist, and that's how you will ultimately prove you're a director.

That is how you will get hired again as one.

The first attempt, however, is difficult because no one in this business is going to hand a movie to you on a silver platter. You have to go out there and make it happen. Perhaps that's where the *mystique* comes into it. It's an extremely primal enterprise—"I don't know how he did it, but he did it." It's appealing; it's quasi-mythological.

FIND THE SUBTEXT

The two essential ingredients in the director's recipe book are **subtext** and **point of view**. First, let's start with the subtext. That is the principal buzzword: the subtext is what you must uncover when you set out to shoot. Subtext is the meaning of a scene that's not readily detectable on the scene's surface.

In screenwriter William Goldman's book *Adventures in the Screen Trade*, he writes in regard to subtext: "If you, as a writer, aspire to quality, it must be alive under every page you've done. Look at what you've written: If all that's going on in your scenes is what's going on in your scenes, think about it a long time." The idea of subtext is also appropriately explicated by Ernest Hemingway's *Iceberg Theory*, which asserts that the meaning of a piece of writing should not be immediately evident, the meaning should lie below the surface, just like the majority of an iceberg lies below the surface of the sea.

People almost never say what they mean. In fact, people often say the opposite of what they mean. This isn't always the case in reality, but it's the core of dramatic writing for theater, film and television.

In a perfectly written script, every single line of dialogue should run against the grain of the character's behavior as written in the action paragraphs. Character is defined by the actions a character takes, not by the words a character speaks. It is the surface that lies. **It lies to protect the subtext, the truth, from being exposed.**

Think of how many times we lie, consciously or unconsciously, over the course of a day. How many times are you actually feeling "good" when someone asks you "How're you doin'?!" Although, the response is always the same: "I'm good...how are you?" It's the surface response, because the subtext is often much too complex to convey via a simple verbal idiom.

So much goes unsaid between people, even between the closest of people. Most people communicate volumes to each other without ever actually saying a thing, and it's that thing that goes unsaid that we attempt to capture on film.

Theatre 101: Drama is conflict. This golden rule is the secret to creating subtext. The dramatization of *inner conflict* in film is realized through the subtext created when the camera is directed beyond the faces of actors and into their thoughts and feelings within.

TIP ▶ COMPLETE THIS ENLIGHTENING HOMEWORK ASSIGNMENT.

Rent and watch David Lynch's *Mulholland Drive*, which is a bona fide lesson on subtext. In the film, Lynch directs the same scene twice; it's as though he's trying to show an audience not only what subtext is, but also why it works, dramatically.

Naomi Watts plays Betty, an aspiring actress who just moved to Hollywood. She has taken in a stranger, Rita, played by Laura Harring. In the first version of the scene, Rita helps Betty rehearse a scene she is preparing to audition for. In the scripted scene, Betty plays a young woman who is having an affair with her father's best friend, the role that Rita takes. Betty confronts her father's friend and attempts to break off the relationship. When he refuses to end things, and furthermore refuses to leave when she tells him to, she threatens to kill him. The scene concludes with Betty bringing a knife to Rita's face saying, with big emotion, " I hate you...I hate us both."

Granted, this is a rehearsal; however, Betty plays what the words are telling her to play: she *hates* this man. The dialogue is being reflected, literally, in her actions, manner of speech and intentions.

When Betty auditions for the role later in the film, in the second iteration of the scene, she plays opposite the actor who has been cast for the role. She performs the same role, runs the same scene and delivers the same exact dialogue. However, the scene is completely different. Why is this the case?

Betty is playing the opposite of what the words are telling her to play: she *loves* this man. She threatens his life not by waving a knife in his face, but by kissing him and holding the knife behind his head.

In the first scene, she is playing the text. In the second scene, she is playing the subtext. When she plays the text, the dialogue handcuffs her performance. She is literally playing one with what she is saying, and this, by definition, is one-dimensional. When she plays the subtext, her dialogue runs in contrast to her actions, her emotions seem authentic, and her performance is suddenly multidimensional.

Human beings are conflicted creatures; drama strives to capture this conflict in a performance. That's what makes a performance ring true to the person watching that performance.

Your homework assignment is to watch both of these scenes in *Mulholland Drive* back-to-back and determine which one works better.

THE DIRECTOR'S TOOLBOX

If all the elements onscreen say the same thing, there's no tension, there's no conflict. And without conflict, we have no drama. **If the words say the same thing as the behavior of a character, there's no truth; or, at least, very little. It aspires to artifice, not art. It's not character; it's cardboard.**

Here are the tools a director has at her disposal, which when combined together, or run in contrast to each other, have the ability to create the appropriate subtext:

TOOL	ELEMENTS OF THE TOOL
Camera	Angle Lens/Filter Movement Frame Focus Speed
Lighting	Color Brightness Hard/Soft Light Direction Contrast
Wardrobe	Color/Saturation Texture Silhouette/Shape Era/Social Status
Actor	Gender Type/Physicality Persona (Known/Unknown) Experience
Production Design	Environment/Location Props Space
Shooting/Editing	Linear Non-Linear
Sound	Music: Score or Source Determining What/Who We Hear Sound Design/Effects
Staging/Blocking	Characters' Physical Actions/ Reactions
Dialogue	Voiceover Explanation (Exposition)

The above elements are to the filmmaker what a palette of paints is to the painter. Each and every one of them should be considered as you break down and visualize the script, as well as when you're in production, in case something isn't working in a scene. If something isn't working, and you can't put a finger on what it is—whether it's the performance, the camera angle, the area of the location, etc.—try reversing one or more of your aesthetic choices. If the actor isn't nailing his or her close-up, shoot the actor from behind or in silhouette; let the withholding of expression work its way into the imagination of the viewers.

Weir and Subtext: *Witness*

In a scene from Peter Weir's *Witness*, Harrison Ford plays John Book, a detective who just received news that his partner has been killed, and not only that, but also that the people who killed him— corrupt police officers in their department—are likely coming after Book next. The moment Book hears on the telephone that his partner was killed, Weir cuts from a close-up of Ford's face to a shot of the back of his head. As Book absorbs the news and hangs up the phone, he gradually hangs his head. Perhaps counterintuitively, Weir refuses to show us Ford's emotion in a close-up. We are left to sketch the emotion on his face in our minds. We are just as physically removed from the information he is receiving as he is as he receives it. He doesn't get the news face to face. He gets it through the telephone, just like we do: we only hear it, as he only hears it.

The shot conveys gravity, literally and metaphorically. Without the distraction of reading the emotion on his face, we focus more on the weight of the situation he's in, a weight that we are made acutely aware of by the lowering of his head. There is no dialogue in this scene that says *the corrupt cops are coming after him*. That is implied. That is the subtext beneath the surface of the text. What better way to convey this subtext than to shoot the character who is being hunted from the perspective of the hunter, the one who will be coming up behind him and trying to take him out?

For the rest of the movie, John Book will be looking over his shoulder, waiting for the bad guys to catch up to him, and how does Weir end this shot? **Ford finally turns around, looking *over his shoulder,* as he comes to this realization. That is how a director shoots the subtext.**

You don't always have to film an actor's face to convey the emotion you want to convey; if you're not getting across what you want to get across in a close-up, try doing the opposite. It just might be the better choice.

Building Subtext with the Right Tools

On the micro level, every tool that's available to the director should be used to generate as much conflict between the elements as possible. If everything in the scene is pointing in the same direction, the scene will be emotionally one-note, and therefore, fraudulent.

For instance, a character may not have any lines in a particular scene, but he looks quite sad. He's so sad he's crying. Then, if that wasn't enough, the director chooses to set the scene on a gloomy night, shooting the actor from an expressionistic low angle, and scoring the moment with a single morose violin. In addition to the crying, the character is consequently bathed in darkness, absent of any hope that the light of the sun, or a lamplight, or even a flashlight might lend. The camera is so low that the actor appears hunched over it, as though he's sharing his burden with us, not to mention the proximity to the falling tears: the lens can almost catch them. And the score is doing the same job as some melodramatic writing might do, if there were lines of dialogue in this scene. The violin telegraphs the character's emotion right down to the second he slits his wrists.

An actual melody requires many different notes in order to articulate an emotional truth. If you hit the audience over the head with one single emotion, echoing it in every element of your filmmaking tools, it will register as false. It will come off as heavy-handed and one-dimensional.

At best, you're doing all the work for the audience; at worst, you're manipulating them into experiencing one specific feeling. Life is not that black or white, and neither is drama. Recognizing subtle shading, as well as the conflict of black and white elements, should eventually lead to harmony on a fundamental level.

Scorsese and Subtext: *Taxi Driver*

In a perfectly conceived film, every shot should be a visual metaphor that conveys the subtext of the written scene.

In the film *Taxi Driver*, there is an uncomfortable scene in the middle of the movie when Travis Bickle calls Betsy, the woman he is courting, from a pay phone in the lobby of his apartment building. The trouble is, when he took her out on their first date, he took her to see a porno flick.

Ever since that rendezvous, she hasn't been returning Travis's calls. Travis isn't a bad guy, but he's out of touch with his society's reality, perhaps due to his stint as a soldier in Vietnam. When he finally gets Betsy on the phone, he makes an effort to apologize and ask her on a second date. Even though we're experiencing the film through Travis's point of view, Scorsese employs some dramatic irony: he assumes we are aware of the societal standards that Travis is unaware of.

The camera is positioned behind Travis—as though we're eaves-dropping on the call. We know the conversation is not going well, and we don't even need to hear Betsy's side of the exchange; we realize the conversation is over well before Travis does. Scorsese encapsulates this idea in a visual metaphor by tracking the camera away from Travis's back, and then dollying it horizontally along the hall, until the shot ends at an intersecting hallway that leads to the building's exit. Even though the camera no longer frames Travis (it now frames the door at the end of the lonely corridor), we continue to hear Travis talk to Betsy over the phone. By directing our eye away from Travis and onto the exit, we no longer focus on the intent of the conversation, but rather on the futility of it.

Scorsese has successfully translated a human emotion to his audience. We feel embarrassed for Travis. We can't help but feel awkward as we witness him try to connect with someone who we know very well he'll never be able to connect with. It's so awkward that we want to stop eavesdropping.

As a result, Scorsese walks us away from the phone before Travis walks away from it, because we know the conversation is over before he does—and if it was us in that scene, we would have probably gotten the hint earlier and walked away at this very same moment. There is an inevitably about this conversation: Travis is going to lose. We know it, Scorsese's camera knows it, and we're both ahead of the character, so we might as well wait for him by the door, because we know that's where Travis is eventually going to head. And Scorsese puts us there. He is filming the subtext of the scene.

FINDING THE SUBTEXT IN YOUR SCENES

A good exercise when you're storyboarding, or at least beginning to think about the shots in your film, is to try to boil each scene down to one shot. If you were only allowed one shot to shoot an entire scene, what would that shot be? The answer is you film the subtext of that scene, and if you do this successfully, you may not need any other shots to convey what the scene is about. This was true for Scorsese in the example above. He chose one shot to convey the subtext of an entire scene, and it was the correct shot. If you plan on shooting additional shots (also known as *coverage*), once you have determined what the subtext is and film THE SHOT that conveys it all, you can use that shot as the spine for all the other shots in the scene.

If you can determine the one perfect master shot for the scene, deciding what coverage to shoot—such as shot/reverse-shot close-ups—becomes exponentially easier. This may seem like a cheat, or a shorthand trick, but I assure you it's not: if you're having trouble figuring out the master shot in a scene, set one or more of the tools above in opposition to another.

Hitting the same note in different departments will lead to redundancy and the viewer will inevitably lose interest in the material. Think about it, why do viewers watch movies? We watch to become invested in characters who are trying to resolve some kind of conflict, and we volunteer to go on that journey with them. If there is not enough conflict in the myriad ways you design the film as director, then the central conflict the characters are seeking to resolve will become tedious, uninteresting and lifeless.

The more conflict in the script and in the visual elements that you choose to bring that script to life, the more engaging your film will be.

ADDING A POINT OF VIEW

The second, and equally important, ingredient to effective directing is the *point of view* (POV) in a film. Wherever the director points her movie camera on set implies a specific perspective. The camera establishes the looking glass through which the audience is permitted to peer; therefore, it creates a point of view. The opening scene in Steven Spielberg's *Schindler's List* as a masterful example of point of view in visual storytelling.

The subtext is what the filmmaker sets out to shoot, and point of view is how the filmmaker shoots it.

Spielberg and Point of View: *Schindler's List*

Oskar Schindler is a German entrepreneur who capitalizes on the Nazi war effort during World War II by acquiring military contracts and hiring Jewish prisoners to make field kits for soldiers on the front line. As the war progresses, and the atrocities toward Jews increase, Oskar finds himself at odds with both his country's role and his role in the war. As a result, he attempts to save his Jewish workers by buying them out of concentration camps and employing them in his factory. When the war finally ends, his Jewish workers are set free, leaving him a hero to his employees, but a war criminal in the eyes of the world, who see him as a Nazi collaborator.

The opening scene is our introduction to the main character. Oskar Schindler is a charismatic businessman who bribes his way into a party for Nazi officers. He mingles with the officers, buys them food and drinks, and has pictures taken with them. Oskar wants to establish relationships with these men and insert himself into their good graces in the hope of acquiring contracts to manufacture supplies for the German armed forces. Spielberg starts the scene at Schindler's home with close-ups that depict the various stages of Oskar's meticulous preparation for the evening. He takes a drink, lays out his clothes, puts on his cufflinks, ties his tie, takes out several wads of money and pins a Nazi Party pin to his lapel. Although these shots are not seen directly from his eyes, the intimacy of the framing suggests that they are from his direct point of view. We never once see his face.

We then move with Oskar as he walks into the restaurant where the party is. The camera tracks behind him, and we see what he sees in *first person* as he bribes his way through the front door and approaches a table. When he sits, the camera swings in front of him, revealing his face. Spielberg briefly SHIFTS back to *third person* POV by framing Oskar behind a pane of glass as a waiter asks the host, "Do you know who that is?" The host responds, "I don't know," and at that point in the story, the audience does not know who he is yet either.

We then SHIFT back to Oskar's POV. In numerous *first person* shots (tight close-ups of his eyes juxtaposed with wider shots of where he is looking), we see Oskar surveying the area, observing Nazi officers and a photographer who is taking pictures of them. Spielberg then brings our attention to an empty table in front marked "Reserved" that Oskar intently focuses on.

When Oskar picks out a particular officer and sends drinks over to his table, we SHIFT to the POV of that character. We now see Oskar in the background from the perspective of this officer as he tries to figure out who Oskar is. When he stands and moves toward Oskar, Oskar meets him and escorts the officer and his girlfriend and the POV back to his table. This dramatic beat ends when the photographer snaps a picture of Oskar and the officer, solidifying their relationship on film through the POV of the camera lens.

The scene's POV continues in *first person* as we jump cut to Oskar throughout the evening watching more and more officers accumulate at his table, enjoying themselves at his expense. When the Nazi Commanding Officer enters the restaurant, Spielberg SHIFTS to his POV as he walks to his reserved table—*the* reserved table. As the Commanding Officer turns around to focus on the commotion taking place in the back of the room, we see Oskar as the center of attention. He's the quintessential life of the party.

The Commanding Officer asks the host the same question the waiter asked of him before, "Who is that man?" However, this time, the host responds exuberantly, "That's Oskar Schindler!" This is the first time in the film that we hear his name uttered. After Spielberg reveals Oskar's identity in this moment, he cuts to a series of snapshots in which Schindler poses for photos with all the officers, and lastly with the Commanding Officer, whom Oskar has been waiting all night to meet, through the POV of the photographer's camera lens.

This is a scene about perception, and Spielberg reinforces this theme throughout the entire arc of the scene by SHIFTS in point of view. It moves from Oskar looking at everyone to everyone looking at Oskar. In the beginning, this man is a nobody, and by the end, he is "Oskar Schindler!"

SUBJECTIVE vs. OBJECTIVE POV

There are basically two types of point of view in film: subjective (first person) and objective (third person). There are also variations of each that a filmmaker can employ.

First Person Point of View

First person point of view is *subjective*: we see the story or action through a character's eyes. This can be done literally where the camera uses a POV shot, or it can be more subjective, conveying how the character is feeling emotionally to the audience.

Some of the variations used in first person POV are:

▸ First Person Singular (the story is told through the POV of one character)

▸ First Person Multiple POV (there are several characters who become a first person POV throughout the story)

▸ First Person Narration
  ◦ Present Tense (in the moment)
  ◦ Past Tense (after-the-fact, looking back)

I'm a big fan of *literal* first person perspective, which establishes a direct POV through the eyes of the main character. *Lady in the Lake*, directed by Robert Montgomery in 1947, is the first example of a film that uses this point of view for the duration of the film. More recent examples of this aesthetic, used to wonderful effect, are in Gasper Noe's *Enter The Void* and Julian Schnabel's *The Diving Bell and the Butterfly*.

Whichever variation of first person is employed, each shares the same thing in common: it is a point of view that seeks to put the audience in the shoes of the protagonist by conveying the emotional reality of the protagonist.

Third Person Point of View

Third person point of view is *objective*: the audience witnesses the events and emotions of the characters from a distance (sometimes referred to as "fly-on-the-wall" or the "God" perspective.) Variations include:

- ▸ Singular (there is only one character)

- ▸ Multiple (there are several characters who we follow in the story)

- ▸ Third person narration

Third person, in its most conventional sense, is in line with Realism. It is also true that many third person movies still tell the story from one character's perspective, although the *camera's* POV is detached. *The Godfather* is a good example of a third person narrative. While on the surface *The Godfather* may depict the inner workings of the Mafia, underneath it's a story about family. We see moments from each family member's life; however, Coppola chooses to shoot this story primarily through the point of view of Michael Corleone. While Coppola's "realistic" style does incorporate different sub-points of view of other characters in the film, it is unequivocally Michael's film:

1. We relate to his character the most.

2. We experience most of the film through his story threads.

3. He is the only character who boasts a complete character arc. He goes from innocent war hero at the beginning of the film to Mafia kingpin by the end.

Third person is arguably the most common type of POV used in films; however, this doesn't mean a filmmaker can't switch POV's in his or her movie to enhance the drama of the story. In my example of *Schindler's List*, Oskar is unquestionably the lead character, and the film is cemented in his point of view, but in the opening scene, Spielberg bounces the POV from Oskar to others around him—the waiter, the officer across the room, that officer's girlfriend—to convey the idea that *others are looking* at his main character, which is ultimately Oskar's objective in the scene.

TIP ▶ IT'S IMPORTANT TO LEARN THE RULES
BEFORE YOU BREAK THEM.

A filmmaker can shift from a first person POV to a third person POV in a film, but can a filmmaker merge first person and third person into the same POV?

In Spike Jonze's *Being John Malkovich*, a through-the-eyes POV shot is used when John Cusack's character, Craig, becomes John Malkovich. Jonze uses the shot to show, quite literally, Craig inside of Malkovich's body. He peers out of Malkovich's eyes and sees the same things Malkovich is seeing. On the surface, this may seem like it is a clear case of first person point of view; it can't get anymore subjective than the through-the-eyes shot, can it?

A student of mine recently challenged this notion. I will paraphrase his argument, citing the scene when Craig first enters Malkovich:

Craig finds a small door in his office, which he can't help but open. He crawls inside and discovers a small, dark, muddy tunnel, at the end of which is the entrance to John Malkovich's mind. While inside Malkovich's mind, he observes what Malkovich observes; Craig is observing the world through someone else's eyes.

Craig is unable to interact with his surroundings; he is simply a spectator inside Malkovich, passively watching Malkovich's life play out in real time. The voice and the actions are of John Malkovich, not of Craig. Malkovich is the one who guides the action, but he is not really the protagonist. In fact, he is not even aware of Craig; his role in the story, at this point, is superfluous at best. Furthermore, the image is vignetted—it's as though Craig sees a portion of the tunnel in his peripheral vision. The sound is also muffled, conveying the feeling that Craig is farther away from Malkovich than he seems. Craig's peeking into Malkovich's POV, but he's in the tunnel while he's doing it—he literally has tunnel vision. Jonze makes these directorial choices to further emphasize the fact that, while it may seem like we're looking through Malkovich's eyes, we're really looking through Craig's eyes looking through Malkovich's.

By its definition, a literal POV shot is not an objective point of view. It is subjective. However, in this scene, the POV shot is not of the protagonist, Craig, it is the POV shot of John Malkovich. Craig just observes what Malkovich sees in third person, which suggests the shot is objective, not subjective. Craig is the character who discovers the door, enters the tunnel, gets inside of Malkovich and is eventually thrown into the New Jersey Turnpike at the end of the scene. It's Craig's scene. It's not Malkovich's point of view, even if it is his POV shot.

Do you agree or disagree?

For a crash course in POV, take a look at this scene. Then take a look at the remainder of the POV shots in the film and see if they evolve each time they're used, becoming incrementally more subjective as Malkovich becomes more physically and emotionally involved in the story.

Before you film, you need to first understand what point(s) of view you want to use to tell the overarching story. Once you know whose stories you want to emphasize, it will be easier to shift the points of view in individual scenes and make sure your audience stays connected to particular characters.

SUMMARY

The director's got a lot of tools to play with, but they require some deft manipulation. As when building a house, a film requires a lot of structural work that may not be immediately visible on the surface, but that make a film more substantial. Go beyond the superficial and explore the inner lives of your characters and the subtext of your story. By experimenting with point of view and the variety of tools at your disposal, you can add depth and dimension to the narrative and the images on the screen.

CHAPTER TWO

THE BIG BINDER:
AKA
"THE DIRECTOR'S BINDER"

The Big Binder is the filmic equivalent to a bible, a production bible, which I should handcuff to my wrist and drag with me everywhere while I make a movie. It is a 2½ inch, three-ring binder filled with all the materials that I need when directing a film. All of my preparation, prior to stepping onto set, is reflected on the pages inside this binder; its importance cannot be overstated. It is divided into 8 sections.

SECTION 1: SCRIPT

The first section is the latest version of the script—including any revisions, additions and exclusions of scenes—printed on one-sided paper. On the side of each page, I demarcate the beats of the scenes by bracketing them with a ruler and a pencil, and then labeling each section by its *Beat Number* (i.e., Beat #1, Beat #2, Beat #3).

What Is a Beat?

A *beat* is a division within a scene in which the action takes a different turn, the momentum shifts, and one or more characters adapt to, or change because of, the shift. With respect to directing performance, the end of one beat and the beginning of another marks the moment that the actor must reevaluate how to portray the character—it's a point when the character must choose a different approach, or *tactic*, on the way towards reaching his or her objective. There are approximately 4 to 7 beats per scene, about 3 beats per page.

Following each page of the script, I insert a two-page chart with my analysis of the beats on the page of script preceding it. I print out this chart and I fill it in with pencil as I break down the script. It includes everything that I need to know in order to direct an actor properly in the scene. The chart is broken down into several columns: Beat, Subject, Circumstances, What Happened the Moment Before, Objective, Obstacle, Action Verbs, Adjustments, the Senses.

Here is my analysis of a beat from the opening scene of my film *Detour*, in which the protagonist, Jackson Alder, wakes up in his car after an accident to find that his car has been buried by a mudslide. This specific action involves him attempting to use his cell phone to call 911:

- **Beat #5**: Jackson uses cell phone.

- **Subject**: Jackson tries to get a signal on the phone to connect with the outside.

- **Circumstances**: Jackson has awoken underground inside of his car following an accident; there is mud completely surrounding him on the outside of the windows.

- **What happened the moment before?**: Jackson was driving to a lunch meeting in the rain on a mountainous road, while pitching one of his advertising ideas to a co-worker on his cell phone.

- **Objective**: To get help.

- **Obstacle**: No signal/reception.

- **Action Verbs**: To ignore; to reach; to connect; to escape.

- **Adjustments**: Dial the phone *as if* you're calling to order a pizza.

- **The Senses**: Gurgling sounds of mud around him; tightness in his parched throat as he swallows; static of the broken radio; stomach is upset; oscillation of brightness and darkness in vision/focus; pounding headache like one might have during a hangover; dizziness; the smell of burnt engine oil.

Using the Beat Chart

This is an extremely physical scene. The emotions are there, but they are not nearly as complex as those explored in the beats later in the film. Jackson's motivation is quite primal in nature. Keeping that in mind, in addition to playing the physical objective and obstacle, there is a deeper aspect to Jackson's character that involves him being in a state of denial. It is clear that neither Jackson, nor most of us at home, have been buried under a mudslide before, so it is reasonable to assume that it may take a while for our brains to compute exactly what that means. So it takes Jackson a few minutes before he can logically understand his circumstances and grapple with the stakes that the circumstances portend.

Jackson is very much in a state of *denial*, and a person in this state may attempt to ignore his surrounding reality, no matter how horrific. He may go ahead and use his cell phone in such a lackadaisical manner that, to the audience, his behavior is more indicative of ordering a pizza than calling the cops. He's not literally ordering a pizza, but if an actor in those circumstances plays it that way, *as if* he was, his performance might solidify the idea of this man being in denial. This is an attempt to convey the idea subtextually, by letting the action of the character in this specific situation speak for itself.

After completing the beat charts, your main goal as the director is not only to identify the ins-and-outs of the scene, but also to have them at your disposal in the event you may have to use them with an actor. Hopefully, you've cast the right person for the role. If you have, ideally, you will need to say very little to the actor in terms of direction.

If you've blocked the scene correctly, defined the circumstances of the scene properly, and if the scene reflects the theme of the film, you may not have to utter a word other than "action" to the actor. But, very often, this is not the case, and you will need to direct the actor. That's where these charts come in.

Beats are the smallest parts of the story. When they're all put together—when performed, filmed, and edited—they should add up to a whole story that has these three overarching plot elements:

1. The character wants something.

2. There is an obstacle that stands in the way of the character getting what he wants.

3. Each time the character tries to avoid the obstacle, he gets pushed farther away from what he wants—until the end when he risks it all, rising above his circumstances and finally getting what he wants (or not getting what he wants, but his life is forever changed because he tried).

SECTION 2: STORYBOARDS

The second section of The Big Binder consists of storyboard drawings for the film. Some directors storyboard, some do not; however, I happen to think it's an essential part of the filmmaking process. **This is a visual medium, so communicating visually is the preferred method.** If you think about it, communicating your shots verbally to others is an extra step that can only lead to a dilution of the concept. The seed of your idea is visual, and then you spend time translating that idea into words, only for it to then be translated back to the visual by your cinematographer, your production designer, your costumer, and the other heads of creative departments.

A *storyboard* is a means of communication through which the unfettered exchange of visual ideas is made possible.

Below is an example of storyboards from *Detour,* which I sketched myself. After I've delineated the beats in the script, I often draw out rough ideas of how I'm visualizing them in my head. Sometimes I sketch them in the margin of the script, but most of the time I use storyboard templates.

Here I illustrate the opening shot of the film, which is Jackson's literal first person point of view. His eyes open as he wakes up to his deployed airbag. As he attempts to orient himself, his bloodied hand comes into the frame. Viewing these beats in sequence not only helps me to brainstorm what comes next, but also allows me to easily share this vision with others.

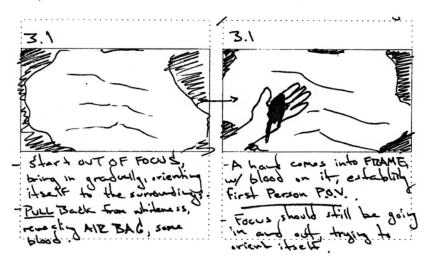

A director does not have to be a sketch artist or a cartoonist to communicate visual ideas (as you can probably tell, I am not either of these things). As long as he can adequately recreate the idea, even with stick figures, it's much easier, and more effective, than trying to verbalize the concept:

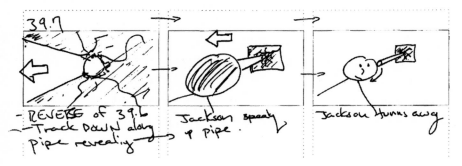

Movies are made to be seen, not to be read. That goes for screenplays, too. People who are new to reading screenplays often find the task insufferable. That is because a screenplay is written to show, not to tell. **Rule of thumb, in the most basic sense, is that if you can't visualize what is described on the page of a script, the writer should rewrite it.** Do not rely on the written word to articulate what is often extremely difficult to articulate. If you do, it can end up like a botched game of telephone, which is no fun to play amidst the strenuous environment of a movie set.

Get right to the point and let your vision speak for itself. I also find that the less artistic the storyboards are, the easier time your collaborators will have interpreting them. Your collaborators are artists, too, and therefore you should respect their interpretations of the visual concepts. If you've already done all the work for them in the storyboards, what have you hired them to do in the first place?

SECTION 3: SHOT LIST

After you've visualized the entire movie, hopefully committing most, if not all, of your ideas to storyboards, then you must do what I just told you NOT to do: translate the shots into words. For me, this is mainly a formality—a necessary formality, but a formality nonetheless.

The storyboards are for your creative team. The shot list is for your producers and first assistant director.

Your producers and first AD (assistant director) don't really care what the shot will look like. They might *care*, at the end of the day, but it's not in their immediate job description or top in the list of their priorities to care. They care about the *logistics* involved in executing the shots. The first AD wants to know how long a shot will take, in order for him to schedule the most efficient sequence of shots per day. The producers want to know what equipment you'll need, and how much it will cost, so they can budget for it appropriately.

Here is an example from my shot list in Scene 12 of the script:

A. Med. of Jackson, frontal, wheel in FG (foreground) as he stares straight ahead.

B. CU (Close-Up) Punch-In of above shot "A."

C. Reverse to what he's looking at: CU of map taped to windshield.

D. SPLIT-DIOPTER shot from behind Jackson. He turns into it, the sunroof is in CU on the *top half* of the frame, and Jackson is framed in focus in the *bottom half* as he looks up at the cracks in the glass.

E. Reverse of shot "D," w/out diopter, Med./Wide filming back of Jackson in FG, between seats, holding their headrests as car begins to shift.

F. Profile Med. of Jackson, hand-held, following his movements as he creates a plumb-line.

G. Profile CU coverage of above shot "F."

H. Wide/Med. of Jackson, frontal, as if POV of windshield, as he ties hanging iPhone to ceiling—Hold this shot as we DUTCH the angle so the plumb-line is level with the lens.

In Scene 12, the producers know I will need a split-diopter lens for one shot and some type of fluid tripod head, or a similar piece of equipment, that allows for the "dutching" (diagonal tilting) of the camera. The first assistant director knows how many set-ups it will take to shoot Scene 12, and which way the camera is pointed in each shot. This allows him to schedule all the shots from one side together, and then when we reverse the camera, schedule the remainder of those shots together.

We were primarily shooting inside a car that could be taken apart, but it takes a significant amount of time to remove the dash and the windshield and relight for the other side. It just makes sense to shoot slightly out of the chronological sequence of the story in order to cluster all the shots together that are being shot from the same side, under the same lighting, and with a particular piece of the car removed.

Shooting in this fashion is standard operating procedure; otherwise production schedules and budgets would balloon. It can sometimes be difficult for an actor to shoot scenes or the beats out of sequence, so part of your job as director is to make sure the performance remains even. Most film actors are used to this type of process, but you still need to keep an eye on it.

Make sure the actor knows where her character has been the beat before the beat she is about shoot, and make sure she is using the appropriate tactic to achieve the objective that will lead her into the next beat.

SECTION 4: SCHEDULE

After you have put together the shot list, the first assistant director will begin to break it apart and schedule it into the amount of days the producer has budgeted for the production. In a perfect world, the producer budgets for the amount of time the first AD schedules for the shoot. In independent filmmaking, however there is often only the bare minimum of money in the bank to make the movie. And this money is usually never enough. For that reason, the first AD normally works closely with the producer to figure out how to fit X number of days in for X amount of money.

Efficiency is the name of the game, because in this world, if you blow everything in production, there's a good chance your film will linger in the purgatory of post-production for an unspecified amount of time.

Here is a sample of the schedule for our shooting day on Wednesday, July 14. The columns break down as follows:

- ▸ Column 1: Page count in the script
- ▸ Column 2: Scene number
- ▸ Column 3: INT/EXT, Day/Night
- ▸ Column 4: Location, time/day reference in script, action
- ▸ Column 5: Which actors are present in the scene

Sheet #:	Scenes:	INT/Day	Location / Action	
Sheet #: 24 — 6/8 pgs	6	INT Day	CAR - TUE 1:55 — Jackson draws a map.	1
Sheet #: 25 — 6/8 pgs	7	INT Day	CAR - BACKSEAT 1:58p TUE — Jackson finds a bottle of water and a granola bar i	1
Sheet #: 26 — 1/8 pgs	8	INT Day	CAR - 2:15 TUE — Jackson climbs into the trunk of the SUV	1
Sheet #: 27 — 2/8 pgs	9	INT Day	CAR - TRUNK — Mud drips in through the roof of the trunk; Jackson	1
Sheet #: 28 — 5/8 pgs	10	INT Day	CAR - TRUNK — Jackson talks about the mud and mud wrestling.	1
Sheet #: 29 — 1 pgs	11	INT Day	CAR - TRUNK — Jackson finds a flashlight.	1
Sheet #: 30 — 7/8 pgs	12	INT Day	CAR - TUE 2:48p — Jackson notices cracks in the sunroof; the car is ti	1
Sheet #: 31 — 1 1/8 pgs	13	INT Day	CAR - TUE 3:02P — Jackson sees an ant; covers the vents with packin	1
Sheet #: 32 — 2 2/8 pgs	14	INT Day	CAR - TUE 3:17P — Jackson starts to panic in the car while filming him	1
Sheet #: 33 — 3/8 pgs	15	INT Day	CAR — Jackson reminds himself to breathe slowly.	1

End of Shooting Day 6 -- Wednesday, July 14, 2010 -- 8 1/8 Pages

The schedule is important for obvious reasons. Of course, you will strive to maintain its deadlines, but it's also good for the actor to have a schedule ahead of time. If the actor knows exactly what's going to be shot the next day, he will be prepared for it.

SECTION 5: CHARACTERS

The fifth section of The Big Binder consists of backgrounds, or biographical sketches, of the characters. The majority of this section involves material that the audience will never confront on screen. It is material that helps the director and the actors understand the characters intellectually and empathize with them emotionally. After all, your characters presumably have lived longer than just the two hours of their lives you choose to project on the screen.

Here is a biographical sketch I wrote for Jackson Alder, which I gave to the actor playing him, Neil Hopkins:

Character Breakdowns

Jackson Alder –

He is the modern embodiment of the classic Thoreau quote: "The mass of men lead lives of quiet desperation and go to the grave with the song still in them."

Jackson is an introvert who makes his living in an extroverted industry, so he needs to work against his own type in order to be a successful ad man. It is this contradiction that simmers and bubbles over in his predicament. It is in railing against his death that Jackson discovers the man that is lurking inside him; in confronting that man he learns more about his true self than he ever knew before.

Jackson grew up in Portland, Oregon and went to school at Bard University where he majored in communications. Jackson met his girlfriend, Laurie, at a music festival in Austin, Texas after they both graduated. Their most favorite vacation was a long weekend at Lake Tahoe where they stayed at the uber-luxurious Resort at Squaw Creek where they did some black diamond skiing. Both Jackson and Laurie are relatively well-grounded—they don't harbor issues or resentments of their parents or other family members. They fully recognize that their issues start and end with themselves—they expect a lot from themselves and from each other and that is the source of tension in their lives. They have been faithful to each other, but both have been tempted by other relationships, as is often the case with the young.

Jackson has an iPhone, but he prefers email, since that means he doesn't have to talk to anyone; he gets stage fright when he has to piss around a large group of people; he gets great energy from the natural world, but prefers the false safety and comfort inside the office world. It is only through Laurie that he begins to open up and realize his love for the outside. Jackson sheds cultural interests—favorite bands, books and movies—like most people shed old socks. He is always trying to find something and never satisfied with what he has. The one and only exception to his prolonged state of disquiet is his relationship with the love of his life, Laurie.

Although never married, Jackson and Laurie are expecting a child and this is the second time Laurie has been pregnant. Their first pregnancy ended in a miscarriage, which weighs heavily on them. It was in the third term and, at the insistence of their family members, they had a full funeral service for their unborn child. This colors the new pregnancy, painting a slightly ominous tone around this otherwise joyous and momentous event. They worry that it will happen again and are inclined to prepare for the worst. They have a hard time enjoying the pregnancy the way so many pregnant couples do. It has the potential of becoming an increasingly emotional burden—they fear that "fear" will keep creeping into their lives, and possibly taint this event.

Preferably, this background information should be as factual as possible. You may touch on the emotional states of the characters, but keep it minimal.

And it is wise to keep the sketches between 1 to 2 pages in length. The actors will have their own methods of preparation, so you will need to allow adequate freedom for their processes—but you should still convey your take on the characters to them, especially if you're the writer as well.

SECTION 6: TOOLS

The sixth section of The Big Binder consists of an array of helpful materials that you might collect while directing the film. For me, this consists of three major things:

1. **Tool Chart**: A chart that reminds me of the elements I have at my disposal to work with, which I described in Chapter 1: CAMERA, LIGHTING, WARDROBE, MAKE-UP, ACTOR, PRODUCTION DESIGN, SHOOTING/EDITING, MUSIC/SOUND, STAGING/BLOCKING, DIALOGUE. Each element should be counterbalanced with the others in an effort to convey the subtext of a scene.

2. **Action Verbs**: I have a list of action verbs that help me communicate objectives to actors, and how they go about achieving those objectives. The list includes variations that provide options for conveying a scene's level of severity.

3. **Color Schemes**: I do not completely subscribe to color theory; that is, red = passion, green = nature, blue = tranquility, etc. However, some interpretations of colors and what they might represent can help you start thinking more in depth about the use of color in your film. Motifs of color can help delineate the arc of a character, whether through the lighting, the production design, or the costuming.

Using Action Verbs

In every scene in a film, characters have goals they set out to achieve: to win an argument; to seduce a woman; to escape the clutches of a captor. In acting terms, these goals are called *objectives*. The means through which an actor goes about achieving these objectives is to use an action verb and express that verb in his performance. Just as you will have your tools, the actor has his, and the action verb is among the most important in his set.

While the actor prepares action verbs for use in his scenes, you should also prepare a list of your own in the event the actor needs some directorial guidance. The list of verbs that I occasionally reference is organized so that I can tweak the intensity of the action and performance. Sometimes an actor takes a verb and either makes a stronger choice than I'd like (perceived often as "overacting"), or makes a subtler choice than I'd like. Some directors handle these two problems by giving direction like: do it "smaller," or do it "bigger." While a good actor may be able to interpret what you mean, and ultimately give you what you want, this type of result-oriented direction is not recommended. Actors act in-the-moment, which means you must direct them in-the-moment, and the verb is your key to guiding them to a natural performance. By having my list ready, I can still have him play the beat's objective using the same tactics, but modified to achieve the correct results.

When actors play a result, rather than using an action verb to achieve an objective, their performances may feel false. They are indicating an emotion, not living the emotion.

The emotions that the actor releases should be byproducts of the techniques she is using to achieve the character's objective. An actor isn't sad because the director instructs her to be sad, but rather she's sad because her character is trying to warn her boyfriend that she's thinking of leaving him, and he's not listening to her. If the actor isn't being persuasive enough, or you think she could use a stronger tactic, instead of *warning*, she could *reprimand* him. If he still doesn't respond, the actor can *teach him a lesson*, in one last ditch effort to get him to respond. If you want her to be more subtle and less intense, she could *give him a cold shoulder*.

If the actor uses the right action verb to drive her performance, the emotion will bubble to the surface on its own.

Here is my list of verbs: the verb in the middle of these sequences is typically the verb(s) you start with and then depending on the level of severity you would like the performance to embody, you can either tone it down by using the verb(s) to the left of the verb you started with, or intensify it by using the verb(s) to its right.

← Less Intense	ACTION VERBS Starting Point	More Intense →
Threaten ◄ Humiliate	Abuse	Beat ► Rape
Criticize ◄ Insinuate ◄ Blame	Accuse	Indict ► Rebuke ► Punish ► Condemn
Shake up ◄ Startle	Alarm	Shock ► Astound
Surprise ◄ Startle ◄ Shock	Amaze	Astound ► Dumbfound
Read ◄ Study	Analyze	Examine
Praise	Applaud	Salute ► Celebrate
Encourage ◄ Build up	Boost	Sanction ► Empower
Weary	Bore	Irk
Pose ◄ Posture ◄ Strut	Brag	Show off ► Flaunt ► Preen
Hassle ◄ Nag ◄ Badger	Browbeat	Harass ► Bully ► Plague
Compliment ◄ Flatter	Charm	Beguile ► Enchant
Warn ◄ Reprimand	Chastise	Teach a lesson ► Punish
Praise ◄ Honor ◄ Glorify	Cherish	Revere ► Worship
Massage ◄ Cajole	Coax	Wheedle ► Sell
Support	Comfort	Cheer up
Grumble	Complain	Gripe ► Whine
Quibble with	Contradict	Negate ► Wipe out
Yearn for ◄ Hunger for	Crave	Wish for

Punish ◄ Hammer	Cripple	Destroy ► Obliterate
Impress	Dazzle	Hypnotize ► Knock out
Duck ◄ Dodge ◄ Shield	Defend	Deflect ► Repel
Confront ◄ Challenge ◄ Goad	Defy	Provoke ► Incite ► Instigate
Ask ◄ Request ◄ Require	Demand	Order ► Exact
Hate	Detest	Abhor ► Loathe
Shrug off ◄ Ignore ◄ Laugh off	Dismiss	Reject ► Tell off ► Terminate
Toy with ◄ Unsettle	Disturb	Agitate
Distract	Divert	Change the subject
Cuddle ◄ Caress ◄ Stroke ◄ Fondle	Embrace	Molest ► Maul ► Rape
Apologize	Eat humble pie	Ask forgiveness
Charm ◄ Amuse	Entertain	Stage ► Perform ► Emote
Check out ◄ Verify	Examine	Prod ► Scrutinize ► Probe
Test	Experiment with	Investigate
Pursue ◄ Entice	Flirt	Woo ► Seduce
Prod ◄ Provoke	Goad	Dare ► Incite
Stalk	Hunt	Chase
Disregard	Ignore	Shut out
Notify ◄ Warn ◄ Caution	Intimidate	Threaten ► Attack ► Kill
Infringe on	Invade	Violate ► Occupy
Request	Invite	Welcome
Berate ◄ Attack (verbally)	Menace	Terrorize ► Knife ► Cut
Toy with ◄ Tickle ◄ Tease ◄ Taunt	Mock	Ridicule ► "Dis" ► Put down ► Deride
Prompt ◄ Remind	Nag	Harangue ► Threaten
Stall ◄ Hold up	Obstruct	Sabotage
Beat ◄ Prevail ◄ Triumph	Overpower	Trounce ► Rout ► Slaughter ► Bring to one's knees
Annoy ◄ Needle ◄ Get one's goat	Piss off	Madden ► Infuriate
Sooth ◄ Pacify ◄ Humor	Placate	Appease ► Surrender to
Ask ◄ Request	Plead	Implore ► Beg ► Beseech
Confront	Pounce on	Ambush ► Nail
Persuade ◄ Coerce	Pressure	Hound ► Persecute
Care for ◄ Nurse	Protect	Mother
Question ◄ Pester ◄ Poke your nose in	Quiz	Pry ► Interrogate

Cloud ◄ Hide	Repress	Suppress ► Stifle
Shame ◄ Scold	Reprimand	Humiliate ► Condemn ► Revile
Daunt ◄ Dishearten ◄ Discourage	Ridicule	Mock ► Belittle ► Scorn ► Deflate
Scuttle ◄ Spoil	Ruin	Wreck ► Obliterate
Enjoy	Savor	Relish
Explore ◄ Delve into	Search	Leave no stone unturned ► Hunt
Mope ◄ Fret ◄ Brood	Seeth	Rage ► Erupt ► Explode
Tiptoe	Sneak	Slink ► Creep
Argue	Spar	Lock horns
Compromise ◄ Accommodate	Submit	Concede ► Capitulate ► Surrender
Coax ◄ Tempt	Tantalize	Lure ► Flirt ► Seduce
Offer	Tempt	Whet the appetite
Reject	Turn your back on	Abandon/Discard
Instruct ◄ Teach ◄ Enlighten	Urge	Lecture ► Preach
Shrink ◄ Diminish	Withdraw	Escape ► Disappear

There are a whole host of other action verbs that one might find useful in directing actors, but the above **cheat sheet** is a good place to start. I always peruse them as I beat out a script and before I rehearse with actors.

Using Color Schemes

One of the most important uses of color is in the wardrobe. In *Detour*, I used the colors of a traffic light to reflect the three main characters in the film. Jackson Alder, whose entire life is transformed when he's trapped inside a car, may have been driven off the road by nature, by fate, by human error, or by some other literal or metaphoric reason. The one thing that is true is that this man started his day on his planned route, but only until he's pushed off of it does his real journey begin.

Jackson's girlfriend, Laurie, is coded with green: the color of nature, the earth, and the color of freedom, permission and "go" in a traffic light. Jackson's unborn baby is red, the color of passion, fire, blood; also the color of "stop" in a traffic light. It is the thing he feels is "stopping" him from living his life.

Jackson, of course, is caught in between both of these colors, caught in between Laurie and his unborn child. He is yellow: the color of the sun, the sun which has become nonexistent in his predicament underground, the color of the sun that only exists via memory, inside of his head—memories that seem so distant, no road could possibly lead back to them.

- Yellow is also the primary color that stimulates mental activity, which is Jackson's bread and butter in his career as an advertising executive.

- Yellow is the first color the eye recognizes when color is presented against black, and black is the principal color of the mud and dirt that presses up against Jackson's car windows, threatening to unleash a torrent of earth into the vehicle and crush him to death.

- Yellow pops out better than any other color. It is the reason yellow is used in most warning signs, like road signs, because the human eye catches it the quickest.

- Yellow is also the color of caution in a traffic light.

I worked closely with my costume designer to incorporate these color motifs into the actors' wardrobes. Color not only helps depict character, as it did in *Detour*, but it is also an important conveyor of mood. I often set aside a few days in pre-production to dig deep into my coffee table books of photographs and paintings to pinpoint specific images that capture the atmosphere that I want to convey in the film. I find that using references of artwork is a good platform on which to base my initial discussions of light, color and space with my cinematographer and, to a lesser but no less important extent, my production designer.

SECTION 7: DIRECTOR NOTES

The seventh section of The Big Binder is reserved for notes the director might make prior to or during production. In the case of *Detour*, I used this section as a place to put my transcriptions of discussions I had with various people who acted as consultants on the film.

One important discussion that I noted was an interview that I conducted with a doctor about the type of physical condition the character of Jackson would find himself in, given the circumstances, and what kind of problems, physical as well as mental, he might encounter as the days progress while trapped underground. These are my notes from the interview:

> **Head Injury** (a concussion is likely in these circumstances, as is the onset of shock):
> - He would probably feel these effects as soon as he woke up:
>   - Dizziness/disorientation
>   - Possibly some blurred or double vision
>   - Diaphoresis (profuse sweating all over the body, e.g., visible beads on face & brow)
>
> - Within an hour post-injury: nausea & possibly vomiting
>
> - Later on: listlessness, sleepiness
>
> - Due to heightened adrenaline his pulse would be racing and it may mask some of his symptoms and pain. However, it is better for him to allow himself to calm down and use the adrenaline-boost to keep his wits about him.
>
> **Oxygen Dreprivation** (most dangerous & severe symptoms):
> - At first, disorientation & agitation (high anxiety level) (The doctor very recently had a patient who kept insisting that she

couldn't remember her own name and was getting very upset about it)

- Second, fall asleep

- Third, death

Physical Appearance:
- All of his ailments would make him pale (lips would be pale as well)

- Profuse sweat within first 24–48 hours and then completely dry from dehydration

- Eyes would get sunken appearance from dehydration

- Lips would have a bluish tint from oxygen deprivation

Information like this is not only important for the actor, as a means of understanding the physical condition of the character and adjusting his five senses accordingly, but also essential for the make-up artist to have. In my film, the make-up had to be subtly modified between each scene to show Jackson's steadily worsening state as the time passed.

SECTION 8: REFERENCES

The final section of the binder is very much a miscellaneous section. It includes whatever else you find helpful and various materials that you would like to have on hand to reference. For example, the emotional skeleton of *Detour* was built upon the bones of Elizabeth Kübler-Ross's Five Stages of Grief, as defined in her seminal book, *On Death and Dying*. I used this information to define Jackson's emotional arc and organized it into this section.

Since Neil's performance was such an immense part of the film, I found that tackling his emotional arc in divisions was a good idea. I separated the script into five subsections corresponding to Kubler-Ross's five stages: Denial, Anger, Bargaining, Despair, Acceptance.

This allowed us greater access into the character's emotional world; it was easier to wrap our heads around the character's journey in parts, whereas dealing with it as a whole might have proved overwhelming. By the end of the film, Jackson must accept his own death before he can attempt to escape; he must be ready to risk his life in order to save it.

Each facet of the production—performance, cinematography, production design, wardrobe, etc.—reflected each stage and the transitions between them. This film is essentially divided up into five dramatic acts, each defined by its respective stage of grief (though differing emotions can overlap into opposing stages; such is human nature).

Other references included in this section of my binder are frame-grabs from other films (films of similar subject matter or of a specific aesthetic), extensive photographs of real mudslides and other natural disasters, and photographs of people who I thought looked similar to, dressed and carried themselves the way that I thought the characters in my film would.

SUMMARY

It may seem like a lot of work, and bulky to carry around, but creating a Big Binder forces you to anticipate every element of the film that you will be making. This saves you, and everyone you work with, essential time and money once you get to the actual production stage. When every cent counts, meticulous preparation can protect you from unnecessary delays and save you when you have unexpected setbacks.

CHAPTER THREE

STYLE AND THEME

Style is often confused with *form*. The *style* of a particular director does not refer to how he goes about shooting something, but rather to the sum result of his storytelling technique—the sum result of all of his creative choices. *Form*, on the other hand, is more structural; it consists of the building blocks of making a movie. Form is how you begin a film. Style, on the other hand, is the finished product that you ultimately construct from all the cinematic tools available to you.

Form
How a director tells his story

vs.

Style
What the final story "looks/sounds" like

THE FIVE BASIC STYLES

I find it helpful to categorize a director's style in the same terms we most often associate with painters, even though filmmaking is unique in that it merges the art forms of literature, photography, sound, and music. The director, the artist, paints a world of sight and sound using a palette with an absolutely astounding amount of colors, shades and textures to choose from.

These are the fundamental five styles, along with some of their practitioners:

- ▸ **Realism**: Style that attempts to represent the Subject(s) exactly as they appear in life, without artifice or unrealistic artistic license. This approach is often referred to as "objective" film-making. Practitioners: Vittorio De Sica, Francis Ford Coppola, Robert Altman, Michael Haneke, Alfonso Cuaron (who is also, at times, an Expressionist)

▸ **Expressionism**: Style that seeks to outwardly express the inner feelings of a character, or characters, as he experiences the story. The approach focuses on depicting the emotional reality, not the physical reality, of a character (it most often involves one sole character who the filmmaker chooses to illuminate perspective). It is often referred to as a form of "subjective" filmmaking. Practitioners: Martin Scorsese, Brian De Palma, Quentin Tarantino, Jane Campion, the Coen Brothers, Nicolas Winding Refn

▸ **Surrealism**: Style that seeks to recreate the look and feeling of a dream. It began as an anti-art movement in the 1920s that bridged the gap between dreams and reality. While Expressionism allows the emotion to express itself, Surrealism allows the unconscious to express itself. This is also a subjective mode of filmmaking. Practitioners: Luis Bunuel, Salvador Dali, David Lynch

▸ **Impressionism**: Style that conveys experience by capturing fleeting impressions of reality or mood. The Impressionist painters, like Monet, Cezanne, and Degas blurred the lines between subject and background in an effort to resemble a snapshot: part of a larger reality captured as if by chance, but not the way a snapshot is printed as a photograph, but the way a moment is perceived and then remembered in the mind. The overall theme, or point, of an Impressionist movie might not become fully clear until the viewer has watched the entire movie, then "stepped back" from it to consider it as a whole (like one might step back and consider a Monet painting). Practitioners: Terrence Malick, David Gordon Green, Lynne Ramsay

▶ **Abstract/Avant-Garde/Experimental**: An "anti-specific" style that focuses on the "unrecognizable." This approach mainly uses color and shape to create compositions and resulting juxtapositions that cannot otherwise be created through conventional means. This approach is purely subjective and seeks to convey emotion through the use of unorthodox visual language. Practitioners: Stan Brakhage, Ken Jacobs, Chris Marker

Finding a Voice

The term "style" can also be referred to as the filmmaker's *voice*: the way a filmmaker sees the world, his own unique perspective on life, and his perspective on story. Every story has been told before, but what's different (and original) about each story told is the unique personal perspective from which the storyteller tells it.

Let's look at Martin Scorsese's style. Scorsese is an Expressionist. Scorsese's movies are reflections of his past and his personality. He draws a lot of script pages from intimate experiences and curiosity—specifically from his time growing up in New York and inside Catholicism. That doesn't simply apply to subject matter. It also applies to tone. In an interview with Roger Ebert, Scorsese said: "I'm not interested in a realistic look—not at all, not ever. Every film should look the way I feel."

Never set out to achieve a style. Set out to achieve the telling of a story and make the proper choices that serve the telling of the story best. This is a trap most beginning filmmakers fall into. We admire other directors' styles and we set about imitating them. This is a terrible thing to do; not necessarily because it's cribbing from others before you, but because it's a sure sign that you are forsaking your story for style. Ultimately, the story dictates the style of the film, not the other way around.

CASE STUDY: PAUL THOMAS ANDERSON

Paul Thomas Anderson is a great example of a filmmaker whose style is constantly evolving and therefore cannot be summarily defined.

On the basis of style alone, you compare *Boogie Nights* to *Punch-Drunk Love* to *There Will Be Blood*, and you will be hard-pressed to determine that the same director made all three films. Each film looks as though someone else directed it.

Boogie Nights, on the surface, is a melting pot of shots and techniques reminiscent of those employed in the films of Scorsese, De Palma and, to a lesser extent, Tarantino. The end of *Boogie Nights* is a direct homage to the end of *Raging Bull* (which is itself an homage to *On the Waterfront*).

The point is: *Boogie Nights* is absent of a style that is uniquely "Anderson"—at least a style that Anderson can call completely his own. Anderson seems to find his voice, and gets close to the heart of his character(s), in the house robbery scene toward the end of the film. He juxtaposes an incredibly chaotic environment—Russian Roulette, firecrackers in the air, Rick Springfield's "Jessie's Girl" blasting on the stereo—with an extraordinarily long close-up of Mark Wahlberg as his character absorbs the situation. While the static form of the shot contrasts with the disorder unfolding around him, his performance intimates that he's dealing with an even greater chaos inside of his own mind. At the conclusion of the scene, it becomes clear that Wahlberg's character must extricate himself from the disorder his life has become in order to harness the emotional stability he needs.

In this scene, Anderson begins to touch on a theme that he will revisit in every one of his movies—a consistent definable theme that he explores differently in each film.

Punch-Drunk Love: Finding Order Amidst Chaos

Anderson seems less concerned with achieving a consistent style in his work than about telling a specific story the way he thinks the story is meant to be told. I think this is the correct approach.

In *Punch-Drunk Love*, Anderson depicts his character embarking on a veritable journey from chaos to order and harmony. Barry's inner life is pure chaos. He is a seething cauldron of male inadequacy, debilitating insecurities and uncontrollable anger. Anderson expresses his character's inner turmoil outwardly through his camera, his lighting, his actor's physical movement, his sets/production design, his costumes, his props, and his sound (score and onscreen sounds). His style verges on symbolism (e.g., the "harmonium" that arrives at Barry's front door in the middle of a horrendous car crash). The need for harmony in Barry's life—symbolically represented by the harmonium—is manifested physically by his love interest: Lena.

The arc of Barry's character is defined by his decision to leave his chaotic world, which he's grown complacent living within, and take his life in another direction as he follows Lena to Hawaii. In doing so, he is pursuing, and consequently achieving, the harmony his life has been craving. This is, appropriately, the midpoint of the film— the moment in a movie when the main character often chooses to take a path he cannot return from (point of no return).

The Master: Using Repetition

Anderson's film, *The Master*, is yet another departure from the previous styles he's established. (It resembles *There Will Be Blood* more than the others.) However, his theme—order amidst chaos— is still very much at play.

The tangible symbolism that was present in *Punch-Drunk Love* is mostly gone from *The Master*. Anderson combines form and style by employing repetition (repetition of shots, of sounds, of dialogue) to advance his story about a burgeoning religious cult leader (played by Philip Seymour Hoffman) who, on the surface, attempts to help Joaquin Phoenix's troubled young man get control of his life. Hoffman's character uses repetition—the seemingly endless repetition of questions and exercises that are masked as therapy—to break his followers, much in the same way interrogators seek to break their subjects.

Anderson emphasizes this repetition not only through dialogue, but also with images and sounds throughout the film (example: the motif of waves/the sea). The repetition provides subtext: Hoffman's "religion" purports that we have all lived endless, repeated lives, and that to this day we carry the burdens of our past lives' traumas. Our curse is that we're unaware of our past lives, therefore, unaware of the traumas that still subconsciously burden us. Hoffman uses this as the linchpin of his religion: he has the answers, and his followers must do what he says to alleviate themselves of their burdens and come to grips with their past lives.

Furthermore, the idea of repetition that is inherent in this religion is made manifest in the characters themselves: Hoffman is seen inhabiting a different opulent home (a yacht, a southern mansion, a grand European estate) in each act of the film. It's not until halfway through the film that we realize these are not his homes. Just like the traumas/spirits that inhabit our bodies over and over again, Hoffman, the con man, grifts his way into other believers' homes and takes over in parasitic fashion. We get the sense that he will continue on this way—finding new places and followers, getting kicked out, and taking his "show" elsewhere, over and over again.

Arguably, the fundamental principle of religion is finding order (albeit, a higher one) amidst the chaos of the world. The religion in *The Master* is no different. Repetition can often invoke the appearance and/or feeling of "order," but the mere repetition of words and ideas is no substitute for the meaning itself.

Joaquin Phoenix is a typical lost soul looking for meaning; however, the repetition of Hoffman's words and the exercises he is made to perform ultimately do not cure what ails him. Like *Punch-Drunk Love's* Barry, Phoenix is afflicted with chaos, but he does not find his order, his harmony, through Hoffman's religion—even though that is exactly what Hoffman promises: harmony of the soul.

The ending of *The Master* implies that Phoenix is finally on his way to finding harmony after he puts the religion behind him. Perhaps this is something he realizes he must find himself...or perhaps never even find at all, for to find it is an impossibility.

THEME INFLUENCES STYLE

Before you consider *style*, you must consider *theme*, because it's the theme that will ultimately dictate the style. The *theme* is the universal idea that threads its way through a movie, the glue that adheres one scene to the next and then to the next. It's often the lesson we learn at the end of the story.

Identifying your theme before you begin making your film is critical; it's perhaps the most important thing you, as a filmmaker, can do in pre-production. When someone asks you "What is your film about?" you will likely respond with the logline. When you ask yourself as the filmmaker that same question, your response should be the *theme* of the film. **The theme of your film is not the plot (which is usually summarized in the logline), but rather the idea that drives the plot.**

Before considering your style, whether it's Realism or the more subjective Expressionism, you must pinpoint a theme. Once you decide on a theme, you can then go through the script with a fine-toothed comb and figure out how, as the director, you plan to illuminate that theme in every scene of the film. Theme speaks to the very nature of form because it is your job as the director to connect each part of your film thematically.

In an effort to get you thinking about theme before diving into directing—and certainly before you start thinking about achieving a style—I've compiled a list of commonly used themes as a reference:

Broad Themes:

- ▸ Man vs. Himself
- ▸ Man vs. Nature
- ▸ Man vs. Society

Within the broad themes listed above are a variety of more specific themes that a filmmaker can explore. Some of the most common themes and sub-themes include:

THEME	SUB-THEME
Absolute power corrupts	
Addiction	
Aging	Coming of age
	Getting older, i.e., accepting death
Beauty	Outer vs. Inner
Being alone vs. companionship	
Betrayal	
Change of power	
Change vs. Status Quo	
Chaos vs. Order	
Communication	Inability to communicate
	Breakdown
Culture vs. Counterculture	
The cycle of life	
Darkness vs. Light	
Death	Inevitability
	Tragedy that results
Desire to escape	
Downfall	Envy
	Gluttony/Excess/Materialism
	Greed
	Lust/Desire
	Pride
	Sloth/Apathy
	Wrath/Rage
Disillusionment	
Dreams vs. Reality	

Empowerment/Injustice

    Gender
    Class
    Politics
    Race/Ethnicity
    Culture

Faith vs. Doubt
Family   Blessing or curse?
Fate vs. Free Will
Fear of failure
Female vs. Male   Compatibilities
    Incompatibilities
Fight the Power   Antiestablishmentarianism
Fulfillment
Good vs. Evil
Heroism
Honor
Hope vs. Hopelessness
Identity Crisis: Who Am I?
Immortality
Isolation
Judgmental vs. Non-Judgmental
Knowledge vs. Ignorance
Loss of innocence
Love conquers all
Love vs. Hate
Manipulation of –   Others
    Nature
    The System
Motherhood/Fatherhood: Embrace of vs. Fear of
Nationalism
Necessity of work
Optimism   Power or folly
Overcoming   Adversity
    Fear
    Weakness/Vice
Patriotism   Positives vs. Negatives
Power of tradition

Quest for discovery/knowledge
Reality vs. Fantasy
Rebirth
Regret
Religion   Positives vs. Negatives
Responsibility   Personal
                                    Public

Reunion
Revenge
Rich vs. Poor
Role of men/women
Sacrifice of oneself for another
Search for the Self   Accepting yourself
                                    Not accepting yourself

Social Mobility
Strength   Outer vs. Inner
Survival   Will to survive
Technology   Positives vs. Negatives
Time   Reliability vs. Unreliability
                                    Being a slave to time (Time
                                    Travel as a way to resolve the
                                    problem)

Totalitarianism
Tradition: Importance/Burden
Transition of Power
Triumph of the human spirit
War   Positives vs. Negatives
Wisdom of life experience
Youth vs. Maturity

The Godfather: More than Mafia

As I mentioned earlier, *The Godfather* is about family. That is its theme: family. Perhaps the most famous Mafia movie in history isn't really about the Mafia, but about family. Coppola uses the Mafia as a metaphor, a lens, if you will, through which he examines the dynamics of family.

This is the very reason why the movie is not only extraordinarily popular, but also remains relevant after nearly half a century since its release. Viewers are not relating to the characters in the film because they're in the Mafia, too—quite the contrary. They are relating to the characters because they see their own family dynamics reflected on screen in the way these characters behave and interact with others. Coppola uses the tenets of Realism to convey the dynamics of his fictional family on screen. However, it's not the style through which we are introduced to this family that we remember; it is the family itself we remember. It's as simple and as clear-cut as that.

Finding My Theme

While style ends up being an important part of a well-told story, I believe theme is even more important. The theme of the film is where the filmmaker derives the subtext, and the subtext is what the filmmaker sets out to shoot. In many ways, the style is window-dressing, the vehicle on which the theme is seated and then driven into the hearts and minds of the audience.

The theme in *Detour* is Rebirth. This theme is the tissue that connects each scene of the film together. At its most elemental level, the entire film is a metaphor for digging your true self out of your buried self—and that's exactly what the main character, Jackson, does.

The decision to concentrate on Rebirth as my movie's theme allowed me to focus much more clearly on each element of the film. The man Jackson is at the beginning of the film must metaphorically die before he is able to resurrect into the new, changed man that he is at the end of the film. The tunnel of mud Jackson attempts to escape through at the end was no longer just a tunnel, but a birth canal. It was important that I think in those terms because theme is what gives a movie depth. This is what it means to shoot the subtext.

A director doesn't just shoot the script, he must *shoot the subtext*, and identifying the theme that ties the parts of your movie together is the key to doing so.

SUMMARY

Although many films have a distinctive style, you shouldn't be thinking about style until you've determined your theme. Theme is what ultimately influences the subtext you want to convey, and by first developing that, your film's form and style will begin to take shape. Although you may admire the styles of other directors, it's important that you find your own voice. What is it that you want to/need to express in your film? If you spend the time to work that out, you'll end up with an original film, rather than an imitation of Scorsese or Coppola.

FINANCING AND PRE-PRODUCTION

In the years following film school, I had a handle on what it took to direct a film. Or so I thought.

After several misfired attempts to get my films made, screenplays read and optioned, among other seemingly impossible tasks, my writing partner and I put our heads together and decided to write something that we could make ourselves without the required permission and financial funding from Hollywood. We thought to ourselves: *what could we write that is logistically manageable, something that employs minimal characters, along with minimal shooting locations?* I was always told to write from the heart, to never write with practical motives in mind, like writing in a particular genre because that genre is trending at the moment, or writing a story with a particular production budget in mind. However, we broke our rules this time and began writing a story that could be shot on a shoestring budget.

If it is done right, limitations can absolutely breed creativity. There is no doubt about it. It is often the case that creating something without limitations can result in laziness, whether consciously or unconsciously. Working with restrictions causes you to think yourself over the logistical hurdles, and the mere act of exercising your brain in such a manner only helps to inject the necessary creative energy into all other aspects of the project.

A STORY IS BORN

My screenwriting partner Dwight Moody came up with the idea of a man trapped underground, something to the effect of a man whose house in the hills gets buried by a landslide and he ends up getting stuck in his basement, or inside of his garage. It was a tremendous kernel of an idea. I really liked it, but I also felt there should be more immediate stakes, which lead me to introduce an even smaller location to this situation. A smaller location means a smaller budget, generally speaking, which was something I definitely took into consideration. We then proceeded to fix our sights on the idea of a man trapped inside his car during a mudslide.

One character, one location. That was the start of it all.

The film was originally called *Buried*, and this was years before the Ryan Reynolds' movie of the same title was made and released. Our title consequently became *Off Road*, which then evolved much later into *Detour*. *Detour* is also the name of a film noir from the 1940s and a Gary Busey film from the 1990s, but you can't copyright a title and, as I'll discuss later in the book, it fit nicely.

It took approximately three years of persistent and painstaking effort to get this project moving. The irony of making a film for nothing—outside the auspices of Hollywood, with friends whom you will inevitably beg for help—is that eventually Hollywood will attempt to wrap its fingers around the film's throat and squeeze. That is what happened with *Buried/Off Road/Detour*...

And that's why it took over three years to make, and another two years to get it out into the world.

Writing the Screenplay

What started out as an experiment in guerilla writing, turned into one of our better screenplays. Typically, Dwight and I work closely together on the outlines of our scripts. Our outlines typically consist of sketching out the main beats of the film, that is to say, about 10 to 15 dramatic turning points in the movie. Then, when it's time to churn out a rough draft of the screenplay, one of us takes a solo shot at it. Once that's completed, we knock it back and forth between each other, taking turns with subsequent revisions until finally, after numerous rewrites, the script merges both of our voices. Dwight and I share similar sensibilities, and we write very similarly, so much so that one might be hard-pressed to tell our styles apart. Still, an individual writer's style will always be unique to that writer, no matter how hard he tries to emulate the writing style of another. **Therefore, bouncing the script to each other like a tennis ball, until it's impossible to tell who hit the ball last, is the process we embrace. It works for us.**

Some writers prefer to work on the script together in the same room, hunched over a single computer, typewriter, or notepad. I've heard that this approach works well for comedy writers because they're able to pitch jokes to each other and work out lines in real-time, material that demands a palpable reaction like laughter. Personally, I find I write better when I'm alone; I think I'm more focused and productive working in a solitary environment. I imagine Dwight feels the same. He also lives in Connecticut, so the physical distance between us makes it harder for us to write together. But that's why email was invented.

In the particular case of *Detour*, we decided to deviate from our traditional approach. We bypassed the outline altogether. I don't normally recommend this, and we did have a number of the beats written out before we started writing. The plot seemed very straightforward: a man is buried in his car, and he's got to escape. It's primal, it's basic, and it could be an extremely compelling story if executed properly. We also decided that the character should be an advertising executive.

We like to write characters whose backgrounds run in stark contrast to the dramatic circumstances that they are pitted up against in the story. I think it's important for there to be an inherent irony to a character's predicament.

In this story, we felt it would be most interesting to see a man who excels in his profession because of his intellectual strength be placed in a precarious situation that demands his physical strength. The irony that we focused on was that this character, Jackson Alder, inevitably has to redirect his intellectual prowess in order to help himself figure out a way to escape. The snappy advertising executive has to pitch to himself the hardest sell of his career: that he's going to get out of this mess alive.

Dwight and I decided that I would begin writing the action, setting up the various situations that our character encounters in the car. I would then pass the situations I wrote that day on to Dwight, and he would write rants of dialogue that he imagined the character saying within the framework of the situations. The next morning, Dwight would send me the dialogue and I would combine it with the action. We maintained this routine with steadfast regularity. In three weeks, we had a script. Once we had a complete first draft, we began to knock it back and forth per our usual process, each taking a turn at revising it, and in just over another month we had finished a readable draft.

Finding a Producer

I approached my AFI colleague, and friend, Carrie LeGrand. Carrie produced several of my AFI films. She was one of the smartest and hardest workers in her class, and a natural fit for this project. I explained the film to her as: it's like *Cast Away* in a car. Her response was along the lines of, "That can't be a feature film, can it? One man in a car?" That kind of biting reaction was exactly what made me want to make the film. I knew that if I could make a watchable, entertaining and thrilling film out of this idea, I could do anything—or at least convey to others the impression that I could do anything.

Where the script saved in money, it certainly made up for in its high degree of difficulty to direct. It may be cheaper to film one actor in one location, but such a scenario makes it significantly more difficult to direct the film in a manner that is dynamic, or in other words, in a way that won't bore the audience to tears. It wasn't easy, which meant it was easy to screw up. The way I looked at it, given the project's limitations, the potential return if I succeeded in making a good movie out of this idea was substantial.

THE MILLION DOLLAR QUESTION

At the outset, I intended to make this film for no more than $10,000 in Dwight's garage, using a junker that I would buy on Craigslist and a whole lot of dirt. I'd use an actor friend of mine, who would be willing to work for lunch and endanger his wellbeing, and shoot it with the help of my AFI colleague Rob Kraetsch, who owned his own RED ONE camera package. I had never used Rob as a cinematographer before, but we were friends and had always wanted to work with each other.

I approached the financer who funded one my first shorts, *Confessions of a Dangerous Mime*. Christina Bloom offered to invest $10,000 in the film. She liked the script very much, she believed in the project, and she believed in me as a filmmaker. Since we had worked together in the past, she was also confident that I could pull it off on such a small budget.

I was all ready to go, and nothing was going to stop me. Until, of course, Hollywood reared its head.

Like any good producer, Carrie had given the script to a handful of people she trusted as a means of finding additional sources of funding if, for some reason, Christina's $10,000 fell through or the project needed an increase in budget. Carrie was working full time for a production company and her boss had taken a liking to the script. Carrie and I met with her boss, who expressed to us that he had financers who were interested in investing upwards of one million dollars into the film; however, it was contingent on attaching a name actor to play the role of the lead. My interest was instantly piqued, but it did require that we put the brakes on the project (and the $10,000 that was initially offered to us) in order to see where this new avenue would lead us.

A million dollars and the opportunity to work with a known actor are things that are overwhelmingly tempting for a first-time feature director. I had to make a decision and, perhaps against my better judgment, I halted the train and chose to play this option out.

While Carrie's boss was in the midst of securing the financing and pursuing potential lead actors that the financers would approve of, we had gotten the script to James Van Der Beek through a friend. He read the script and liked it. There were also significant attempts at getting the script to other "known quantities" in the acting world, but these efforts ultimately did not pan out.

Van Der Beek was the star of television's *Dawson's Creek* and the hit film *Varsity Blues*. He wasn't exactly "A-List," as far as quantifying an actor's value goes, but I thought he was a really good fit for the role. *Varsity Blues* was made a number of years ago, but it was a big movie— I have no doubt that Van Der Beek's angst-ridden delivery of his line "*I don't want your life*" is still mimicked at frat parties throughout the Midwest today. The role of Jackson Alder is the role of an ambitious adman who walks between the raindrops, who's never had a bad day in his life—at least a day he hadn't had complete control of—and then suddenly he is caught in this situation that unravels him completely.

James always struck me as a put-together guy, someone who always seems like he's in control. I later joked with him that if I were ever suicidal, I might like to talk to someone on a hotline that had a voice like James Van Der Beek, because he's very calm, but tempers his coolness with a confidence that's impossible to ignore. Someone like that, someone who appears less likely to surrender to panic, is much more fascinating to watch unravel in this pressure-cooker situation than someone who is neurotic and prone to losing it more easily. **There's more of a character arc to this type of individual, which is what you want to convey in a hero.** In most cases, you want to depict your main character as a person the audience can relate to, who when confronted with a set of extraordinary circumstances, is able to reach down deep inside himself and find what he needs to overcome forces that threaten to overwhelm him.

Capitalizing on Van Der Beek's interest in the project, Carrie's boss lined up the investors who were willing to put up the million dollars for the budget if James were to attach himself to the film. The financers approved me to direct the film and were simply awaiting his attachment, or the attachment of a name actor with a reputation equivalent to or greater than James Van Der Beek's. The first part of the investors' requirements seems like a no-brainer—the part about me being approved as the director—but I cannot stress how important that part is.

How to Become a First-Time Director...or Not

The biggest hurdle you will encounter, as you set about a career in directing, is the Catch-22 that is intrinsically involved in the pursuit. **It's not easy to direct a short film, but it is a great deal easier than directing a feature film. The question remains: how do you get to direct your first feature film? And the answer that everyone who asks that question gets: *You had to have directed one already.***

Well, that doesn't make any sense. No, of course it doesn't. If that is true, how did the directors who are currently working in the industry get to be where they are? This is just the way it is. For instance, David Lynch's first feature film, *Eraserhead*, took him eight years to complete, but he made it for nothing and did it himself, along with the help of a few talented friends. Martin Scorsese shot his first film *Who's That Knocking At My Door?* on the weekends. Darren Aronofsky, *PI*; Robert Rodriguez, *El Mariachi*; Kevin Smith, *Clerks*; Christopher Nolan, *The Following*: all made their first feature films by themselves.

The do-it-yourself approach still matters, and it still serves as a legitimate entree into Hollywood.

No one is going to hand you ten million dollars to go make your first feature, even if your short film is the coolest thing since sliced bread. This business is all about risk management. I cannot tell you how many of my meetings ended with executives in the room loving what I had to say, but ultimately being too concerned that I was a "first-time feature director" to take me seriously. I consistently responded to such assessments by stating, "Yes, technically I am a first-time feature director, but I've directed enough shorts to equal the length of three feature films."

I thought it was convincing enough of an argument, but apparently others did not. When it comes to funding films, every investor is looking, and looking hard, for a reason to say "no." It is a habit of risk-avoidance, and employing a director who has never directed a feature film is at the top of their lists as something to avoid.

So, technically being a first-time feature director with a million dollars behind him on his first feature is a significant accomplishment. And, as it turned out, it ended up being too good to be true.

In preparation for my one-on-one meeting with James Van Der Beek, I had created a look-book for him that communicated my vision as director. It included the theme of the film, the tone I wanted to achieve, and the arc of the character. I incorporated selected storyboards that depicted how I was going to visually capture his arc. It also included a collage of photographs/drawings to help him picture the film. Going into the meeting, James had read the script, seen examples of my past work, specifically work that involved minimalist stories and elements, and he had a visual outline of the entire movie as I pictured it. I felt confident that I was as prepared as I could be for the scheduled sit-down.

When I finally met with James—I say *finally* because he did not show up for the first scheduled meeting—we got along like chums. James was polite, smart and very complimentary of the writing. He was even prepared with some great ideas, one of which was to push the moment when Jackson records himself talking to his unborn child until later in the story. This was very insightful, and I gladly ran with the thought. It lengthened Jackson's arc, strengthening the drama and making the character work harder as he evolved from *hesitant* father to *willing* father. We talked through the script, related it to our own personal experiences, and seemed to be completely in tune with each other's creative perspectives on the project. All in all, I thought the meeting could not have gone better. It went so well that, by the end of it, I had completely forgotten about the previously aborted one. I reported as much to my producers and they proceeded to get the ball rolling with his agent.

Approximately one week later, his agent contacted my producers and told them James wanted to meet with them, but without the director present. This request seemed unusual to me, but perhaps James wanted to address logistical matters or safety concerns with the producers. That is how I rationalized it. Carrie and her boss agreed to sit down with James, and when they did, he proceeded to tell them how much he loved the script, how much he wanted to star in the film, and how much he would like *his friend* to direct it instead of me.

Carrie and her boss certainly did not expect this request, but they handled it as best they could in that moment. James gave them a copy of his friend's film (he had directed one feature before, back in 1996) to take a look at.

To my producers' credit, they politely said they'd watch the film, but with the caveat that I was already attached to direct, that they had complete faith in my vision, that the financers had faith in me, and that was not likely to change. My producers ended the meeting cordially, waited a few days and then contacted James' agent. They related the sentiment that their minds had not changed and that, as long as they were involved in the project, I was going to be the only one to direct this film.

Several days later, James' agent contacted my producers again and informed them that James was ninety-five percent committed to the project, that he didn't have a problem working with me, and that he wanted to do the film—but he just wanted to have one more creative conversation with me about the script. I said, sure, have him call me. I still thought that he would be good in the film and help secure the funding we needed. I decided not to take what he tried to do personally.

When James called me later in the evening, I had my script within arm's reach, my PowerPoint visualization of the film open on my computer, and I was ready and willing to talk story. However, it wasn't more than a minute before I was completely sideswiped. He quickly shifted the focus of the conversation from the script, which was what I was told we were going to discuss, and onto me: specifically, my ability to direct this film. Before I could even grasp at what he was getting at, he proceeded to try and convince me that I shouldn't direct it.

"Will, I think that maybe you're too young to direct this film, that you'd be more equipped to direct it in, say, about ten years," he said.

I didn't respond immediately. It took me a while to compute the meaning of his words. I had to think through the words and phrases I was going to use before I responded, as I knew my reaction might very well impact the project. I thought to myself, *James, we're the same age, dude...plus in ten years, you'll be too old to play the part*. I was completely caught off-guard. I was astonished that he would even suggest such a thing to me directly.

There was a period in my life when I suffered from panic attacks, around the time of September 11, 2001. I worked in a high-rise in midtown Manhattan and watched the towers fall in real-time from my office window. For a six-month period following the tragic event, my attacks were severe enough that I would experience a vertigo-like sensation each time I rode the elevator to the upper floors of my building. I eventually stopped having them, but this conversation with James was the first time that I felt that terrible sensation again. I felt it rise from the tips of my toes all the way to the roof of my skull. When this occurs, when it hits the top floor of my biological framework, my throat closes up and I can barely talk. I feel like I'm falling, like the common denominator of gravity has become an endless spin on Space Mountain. I recognized this feeling immediately and I felt it begin to take its hold on my breathing. Intellectually, this incident taught me to always expect, or at least entertain, the worst-case scenario I might encounter in this business.

If you're directing something, always expect that someone wants to take your job from you, and this is because there is always someone who wants to take your job from you.

I must have sounded awkward as I stumbled over my words in an attempt to generate a response, but eventually I did get a grip on myself. James then began to imply that he really wanted to do the movie, and he knew the investors were relying on his commitment—my producers had hinted as much to him in their meeting—so it would be in everyone's best interest that I agreed to the request. He didn't use those exact words, but the implication was clear.

Even though I was exploring other options, seeing what kind of money and resources were potentially out there for this film, I knew I had written this film to make for nothing and I was going to do that if I had to. Realizing that I could still make this film without relying on the traditional channels that most filmmakers depended on, freed me immensely. It was this freedom that I reached down inside myself to grab, and I waved it proudly in front of my telephone receiver. I told him that I was directing this film. That was not going to change, now or ten years from now: I invented the character and therefore I was the best person to direct it. I was the only person who could direct it.

James suggested that I might be happy with just taking a writing credit on this one, because having a produced screenplay credit is an accolade that is worth a lot in this town. He was throwing doubts at me like darts, seeing what would stick into my corkboard of brain matter. But I had nothing to lose. I was going to make this film no matter what, and embracing that thought allowed me to once again take a deep, full breath.

In as polite a way as possible, I said, "James, why would I surrender my directing responsibilities to someone else to just be a writer on this project? It's my film, my producers support me, the financers have approved me, and it's up to me to approve the cast. James, I want you to play this part, but I'll be honest with you, if you can't trust me as a director, you shouldn't play the role."

In my experience, once an actor sees himself in a role, he has to play that role, and I did not think James was an exception to this rule. I told him that we needed an answer regarding his commitment by the end of the week. Eventually, we segued back into discussing the script and ended the conversation by insisting that neither of us would take what was said personally.

I couldn't sleep that night. Not one solitary wink. The sum total of my skills as a director had just been questioned by an actor who was to play a role in a film that revolved solely around his character. In fact, he tried to fire me; actually, it was more like he tried to get me to fire myself. This was a recipe for disaster. The thought that an actor could not trust me to direct him was disconcerting, but we still needed him to acquire the funding.

After a dark night of the soul, I decided that I would try to work with him, that perhaps this tension would be good for the film. The producers went back to his agent and said that we were proceeding as planned, which included me helming the ship, and that we would need a commitment from James by the end of the week.

As the end of the week arrived, I got word that James wanted to speak with me again. I had enough at this point, enough of these exercises in semantics, and I told my producers to tell his agent, "No. I will not be speaking with James anymore. When he commits to the project, I'll speak to him." The producers relayed the sentiment and asked for an answer from James regarding his commitment to the project by 9:00 AM the following morning.

When 9:00 came around and we hadn't heard anything from his camp, we decided that we were moving on. We contacted his agent and said thank you, but we've moved on to other casting choices. In a little under two hours, I received a call directly from James on my cell phone. He told me how much he wanted to do the role and that he completely trusted me as a director. Perhaps the threat of making an offer to another actor helped him suddenly realize that he trusted me.

TIP ▶ LEARN TO COMMUNICATE WITH YOUR STAR.

The one thing film school does not teach you is how to deal with "name actors," i.e., stars. It is simply beyond the school's resources, since most Hollywood hotshots would not be caught dead doing a student film. But it is an extremely valuable experience, because if you plan on a career making movies, you'll have to work closely with the movie industry's elite.

In my experience as a director, I've worked with both film and television stars, and I'm hard-pressed to recommend one definitive strategy for successful communication—except, of course, to spend as much time talking through the script, investigating the character with the actor, and getting on the same page before you both step onto the set. The most important question I pose to the actor in the first meeting is: What is your process? Until I know what the actor's process is (is he a method actor, does she practice the Meisner Technique, does he not like to interact with other cast members and crew between scenes?), I cannot determine how best to approach that person when giving them directions.

You must respect the process of the actor and, in a sense, tailor your process to them (as much as possible). Actors, especially actors with big names, are mindful of their reputations, so arguably it is even more critical for a "star" to be able to trust the director than actors who are up-and-coming. Their reputations are in the director's hands. It is therefore important to establish that trust from the get-go. Ask them what their process is, what they typically look for from their director, and assure them that you'll be there for them every step of the way and that you will not let them fail—that you'll catch them if they fall.

For more in-depth discussion of the relationship between directors and name actors, I highly suggest you read a book called *I'll Be in My Trailer: The Creative Wars Between Directors and Actors*, written by John Badham, veteran director of such films as *Saturday Night Fever* and *Wargames*. It's a great book; it's eye-opening, practical and a super fun read. It should be required reading at film schools around the country.

Financing Follies

With a verbal commitment from James, my producers and I began solidifying the funds for the film. It was at this point that I was told we'd be receiving upwards of $400,000 from a product placement company that Carrie's boss had pitched the project to. This, evidently, meant that we would have to incorporate products into the film that I had not anticipated playing roles in the story.

The props that I had written into the film all had narrative significance: Jackson uses the seemingly benign objects in his vehicle in increasingly inventive ways as a means of escaping his situation. **The props mattered. They were designed to become more and more personified as the film progressed; therefore any prop just sitting around that Jackson doesn't use—especially if it boasted a brand name—would scream *product placement* and consequently take the viewer out of the film.**

This was the beginning of the end for this avenue of funding. Nevertheless, Dwight and I were prepared to incorporate a brand name power drill into the story. But I insisted that the drill could not work—that was my stipulation—because if it worked it would make the character's struggle too easy, and drama is not supposed to be easy. However, he could use the drill *bits* to aid him in his tasks.

The production company had a good relationship with this particular product placement business and Carrie's boss said he had negotiated a deal with them. One of the deal points, which I was told about *after* he had negotiated it, was to write a role into the movie for the wife of the owner of the business. I was clearly surprised he made this deal without consulting me, the writer who would be writing the role, not to mention the fact: ***This movie is about one man trapped in a car. How was I supposed to write another character into a script that was written primarily as a story with one character?***!

It was staggering. But after the fiasco with James, I refused to be surprised by anything anymore. Carrie's boss was bringing money to the project, but the director invariably must set the tone, set the example, and therefore must establish himself as the leader, even if it means putting his or her job on the line. After I admonished our producer for his assumptions, assumptions that would result in altering the story, Dwight and I started to brainstorm writing another role. Even though we were irritated that we even had to humor this request, we actually came up with a scenario that ended up helping the script in the long run.

As I mentioned earlier, limitations breed creativity, no matter how terrible or invasive those limitations may at first seem. There will always be obstacles in making a film, but we must learn to embrace them—we must consider them opportunities to think about our story in different ways and from different perspectives.

The role for this actress, along with other ideas, opened up another dimension of the story that involved dreams and hallucinations and flashbacks via the use of the character's cell phone. All of these ideas ultimately enhanced the story.

During a rather excruciating contract negotiation process, it became more and more clear that the funding the production company was bringing to the table had not been completely there in the first place. I also felt our project was becoming increasingly more compromised as the days progressed. I was not privy to any commitments of funding ever being obtained in writing. I wasn't a producer, much of this was outside the realm of my responsibility and expertise, but I did hear murmurs about deals being made on cocktail napkins at bars. Sometimes this stuff actually passes as professional conduct in this business; however, it often doesn't matter what the means are that finally bring the money to the table.

What matters is whether the money is there when you're about to sign a contract, or whether it's not. The money was not there when we were about to sign ours. **I often quip that a movie isn't real until two things occur: 1) The money's in the bank, 2) The camera on set is rolling. If those two things have not occurred, you must seriously question whether or not you are making a movie.**

Turning to Plan B, or Was It Plan A?

Carrie and I parted ways with her boss's company after spending the better part of a year dealing with them, rewriting the script, and courting a number of actors. James Van Der Beek was still interested, which was beneficial to us as we approached other investors. However, he had become a wild card in my mind, given his skepticism of me as a filmmaker. If I were to hire him to play the role, it would be very difficult to salvage the film if he decided he wasn't going to listen to me. There weren't any other actors to cut to in that car if his performance was not what I wanted it to be. The movie was told entirely through his point of view.

This was a huge risk to take. As the director of this movie, I needed to have a partner in the role of Jackson Alder, not an opponent.

As we explored casting the other few roles in the film, we received interest from Brittany Murphy (*Clueless, 8 Mile*) to play the role of Jackson's girlfriend. The part was small, but extremely important nonetheless. The role of Jackson's girlfriend Laurie was the heart of the film: Jackson's motivation to battle out of his predicament and survive. Through my manager, we quickly got Brittany and her manager to support the project and procured her verbal attachment to the film. With that support, new possibilities for funding opened up. We were revitalized. We created investor packets, highlighting the interest from these name actors, and emphasizing the contained settings and action, which meant in no uncertain terms that just a little bit of money would be turned into high production value.

As we shifted into high gear, we were eventually knocked off balance with the terrible news of Brittany Murphy's death. I received the news on the morning of my birthday, December 20, 2009. I was devastated. I was not friendly with her, but someone dying so unexpectedly and so young is just incomprehensible.

It is perhaps selfish to acknowledge, but our latest possibility for funding had died along with Brittany—potential funding from investors with whom we'd spent close to another year generating interest. I was back to square one.

After just over two years of pursuing avenues that ultimately didn't lead anywhere, I was completely fed up. Sometimes you have to go with your gut, and my gut was telling me that Hollywood, at this moment, was not on my side. Why had I even indulged these possibilities when the whole point of the project was to circumvent them in the first place? This is exactly my point, and it is this point that I am trying to convey to you so that you do not repeat the mistakes I made. **Maybe making these mistakes was a good thing for me, and perhaps making mistakes is a good thing for you; maybe it's akin to enduring a trial by fire.**

I decided to go back to my original plan, to make this movie for the $10,000 price tag that I was initially going to make it for, and I was not going to stop this time. I approached my initial financier

Christina Bloom, whom I had put on the backburner as I indulged my thirst for acquiring greater funds to quench our rapidly inflating budget. She regretfully told me that her money had dried up. It wasn't a surprise, and I couldn't fault her for not setting aside the money for me while she waited two years. We hadn't signed any contracts, and if I had really wanted to use her money, I sure as heck would have used it when it was offered.

Once I had $10,000 and now I had nothing. This person believed in me as a filmmaker; she was willing to invest in me. I had people to help me make the film for nothing, but I was seduced by Hollywood. I went ahead and plucked the apple off its tree and took an enormous bite. Actually, I think the palm tree is a more appropriate symbol, not only for its correlation to southern California's topography, but also for its coconuts. Unlike the apple, when you attempt to bite into a coconut, you'll find it's impenetrable, and your attempt futile, no matter how badly you want inside of it.

That's about as accurate a representation as I can illustrate of what it's so often like trying to break into Hollywood.

MAKING IT ON MY OWN

As I regrouped, saddling up once again and getting the word out that I was going to forge ahead and make this film on my own, we stumbled upon another opportunity for a slightly higher-budget. I couldn't help but feel like I was experiencing *déjà vu*. The latest opportunity came in the form of Ashton Kutcher's company, Katalyst Films, which had just initiated a microbudget department and was actively looking to back a series of movies for a quarter of a million dollars each. My manager had floated the concept around to a few of her contacts, including the head of film production for Katalyst, Bruna Papandrea. Bruna thought the idea was great and loved the script. She brought in the project.

After meeting with Katalyst, I felt like we were on the same page. I had had meetings like this before, but the thing that made this one different was that I made it clear that I was intending to make the movie, no matter what. Whether it had a high budget or no budget, it was going to happen.

Bruna was very enthusiastic about the project, even suggesting that it could be a great vehicle for Demi Moore (I would have to change the character's gender of course, but it could be done if we were hired to do it). However, it seemed clear to me that the company's greenlight of this project largely came down to whether or not I had directed a feature film before. *If I had a nickel*, or so the saying goes. As I realized this, it didn't much matter anymore, since I had made my mind up to make the film regardless of the outcome of these meetings. It still baffled me, though: what established feature director would even consider taking a job making a $250,000 microbudget film? That was the number for the budget they were proposing.

Perhaps the economy was really that bad? In my opinion, they needed someone *exactly* like me to make this film.

I decided to approach a wonderful actor friend of mine, Neil Hopkins, whom I had worked with previously on my AFI thesis film, *Shadowbox*. Neil was not an A-Lister, but he had starred as Dominic Monaghan's drug-addled brother in the hit television series *Lost*, among other notable roles. I had thought about Neil in the role of Jackson, but my attention had sidetracked. I began to realize how terrific Neil would be in the film.

Once I made my decision that I was going to make this film, come hell or high water, I brought the project to him and asked him to star in it. Just like that. I couldn't promise him much money, if any, and he knew I couldn't, but it was an opportunity to star as the lead in a feature film, something Neil had yet to do. Fortunately for me, he was just as excited about the project as I was, and we had worked together before, which minimized potential creative conflicts. I knew how he worked, he knew how I worked, and we both respected each other's process. This kind of collaborative relationship was something I could almost count on not having if James Van Der Beek were to star in the film.

While we were awaiting the final answer from Katalyst, I took the script to Brian Udovich of Rough & Tumble Films. Brian was an up-and-coming producer who produced *The Wackness* and *All the Boys Love Mandy Lane*, in addition to being a fellow graduate of AFI. He and I had several mutual friends, and he had recently read a couple of my scripts that were recommended to him. It turned out he was a fan of my writing and wanted to learn more about *Detour*, since he had heard that I was determined to make it and make it soon. Brian and his producing partner Justin Duprie loved the script, but weren't completely sold on me directing it. They wanted to see some scenes shot.

This is what's known as *proof of concept*, a phrase that was being used more and more in the business during the troubled economy. **These pre-production clips are also called *sizzle reels*, or *teaser reels*. In the eyes of the people with the money, it helped minimize risk.**

Brian saw the potential of a character-driven story masked as a genre film. It was a disaster thriller, but he wanted to be sure that I was capable of generating the necessary drama within such a contained space. It was something he felt as a producer he could make and sell, but he wanted to see something concrete first.

After enduring so many peaks and valleys—though there were decidedly more valleys—I admit I was a bit exasperated by their request. However, it actually turned out to be one of the best things we could have done. Neil and I met several times, worked on the script as I pictured him in the role, and we decided to shoot three scenes that I thought would serve as adequate glimpses into the character's emotional arc and my visual approach to making the film.

We shot the opening scene of the film inside my cinematographer Rob Kraetsch's car, the outside of it taped with black garbage bags as our substitute for mud. Rob was willing to shoot the movie for free, but he'd be damned if he was going to let me destroy his vehicle in the process. (Tip: You can only ask so much of a person.) After we got the scenes in the can, Rob and I edited the footage on his laptop. The scenes turned out great; I felt that much of it was pretty riveting and thought others would feel the same when they watched it. It also hinted at the idea that I had all long, the reason why I wanted to do this: it proved I could make one man trapped in a car not only interesting to watch, but also compelling.

Everyone I showed the clips to wanted to see more, which was definitely a very, very good sign.

I posted the scenes to a secure link on Vimeo and sent the link to Bruna over at Katalyst and brought a DVD to Brian to screen for him personally. I watched it completely through for the first time in Brian's screening room, since Rob and I had literally just burned the copy on his laptop in my car on the way to Brian's office. Brian watched it and ended up loving the footage. I also sent the clips to a few other friends of mine.

One friend in particular, Luc Des Groseillers, a screenwriter who I went to AFI with, saw the footage and offered to invest $15,000 in the movie. Luc is a good friend of mine, and he knew how long and hard I had been working on this. He told me that I needed to make this movie. He gave me the money to get me started. I would not have been able to get this train moving at the speed it needed to move without Luc's support, both financially and personally. He was instrumental and I can't thank him enough.

Once Rough & Tumble knew that Carrie and I had acquired start-up funds and were officially setting a date to begin principle photography, they decided to jump on board and commit resources and matching funds. We also sparked interest from some other producers, which I will discuss later.

STICKING TO A START DATE

At some point around this period in the process, I found time to get married to my girlfriend of seven years, Rachel. We spent a week in New York, where we're both from, had a beautiful ceremony at Tappan Hill Mansion in Tarrytown, an estate that was once owned by Mark Twain, and then came back to Hollywood for our "honeymoon," which was probably not the work-free romantic idyll that Rachel had envisioned.

I was amazed that I was able to take a week off, celebrate with my new wife, and barely had any voicemails or emails from producers. I knew the ceasefire was not going to last long.

When I arrived back in Los Angeles, the dates we had set were exactly one month away. As the deadline approached, Rough & Tumble urged me to push back the production of the film. I instantly felt that the train's momentum had slowed, and maybe it was because I wasn't around to keep steering it toward the impossible.

I realized at that moment that that's what a director does: a director dreams, and a director is often necessarily delusional, but he controls his delusions in such a way as to convince the people crunching the numbers to believe in the impossible. Perhaps the sudden hesitation was part and parcel of this risk management mindset, but Carrie and I didn't see any point to changing the dates. It was a contained film that was written to be shot for nothing, so what were we waiting for? We decided to keep going.

I proceeded with prepping the above-ground scenes, the flashbacks, which were much cheaper to shoot than the action in the car. In fact, by the time we started production, we still had no idea how we were going to pull off the car stuff. But it didn't matter.

This is probably the most important point of all: *set a date and stick with it, whether you have the money or not.* Any working director will tell you the same thing. My directing professor at AFI, Rob Spera, would often tell my class, "If you have ten grand, set a date and move forward. If Tom Hanks calls you on Sunday and tells you he wants to be in the film, if he's not there Monday morning, you're shooting without him."

It's all about *momentum*.

Everything around you, people and circumstances alike, will tell you to wait, to hold off just a little longer, so that the timing will be perfect. The fact is the timing will *never* be perfect. Just place one foot in front of the other, and step into battle. As the director of the film, you have to be willing to make the first move.

I attended a Q&A with Terry Gilliam around this time, and he said the same thing. Someone asked him when he was going to start shooting his next film. Without a second's hesitation, he responded, "April 24th." The spectator followed up her question with another: "*Do you have the funding?*" Gilliam scoffed at the question, responding, "No. Of course not. I never find funding until after I set the date...that's how it all starts."

Catching a Moving Train

Everyone can stand around and wait for the train, but once it arrives, a decision has to be made to get on or not. It's a lot easier to remain passive and not make a decision. William Goldman used to say about this business, "nobody knows anything," and he's absolutely right. Movies are so subjective; no one knows what's going to be a hit and what's going to tank. As a result, unless a person is pushed to make a decision, that person will happily remain mute for as long as he or she can get away with it. No one wants to be responsible for a failure, and since no movie is guaranteed to succeed, it's rare that you'll hear people say "yes" in this industry. You'll more frequently hear "no," or receive no response at all, as opposed to a reply in the affirmative.

It's the director's job to get that train moving, because once it starts moving, collaborators are more likely to get on board. People want to be a part of something that is *happening*, so make it happen.

Several months before the date that we were set to begin, around the time Rough & Tumble became interested in the project, I had passed the script to Diane Becker and Melanie Miller, producers at Fishbowl Films. I had gone to AFI with Diane and had always wanted to find something to work with her on. She had taken a liking to the script, as did Melanie, around the time I spread the word that I was moving ahead with production with or without money in the budget.

I got the impression that if they were to be involved with the project, their inclination was to try to find a "name" to attach in the role of the lead. They felt that since the movie revolved more or less around one person, that the person should be a household name. I felt the opposite. I understood the inclination—it's easier to market a movie with actors the audience is familiar with—but at this point I thought the person should not be a household name. If he was a household name, he'd bring too much baggage to the part. I thought that if we used a name actor who was onscreen throughout the entire film, often without any interaction with other characters, the viewer will inevitably begin to think of the other roles he played. Whereas, if the role was played by someone who was unfamiliar to an audience, viewers would be more likely to put themselves in his shoes and, consequently, go along for the ride. It took me over two years to arrive at this conclusion, but arrive at it I did.

I wanted the film to be a vicarious experience, wherein the audience could see themselves in this type of situation. That's where the thrills were going to come from: *this could happen to anybody*. And the more the audience related to the character, the more they could let themselves, and their accompanying emotions, go.

As Carrie and I moved forward with shooting, I approached Diane with the footage we had shot. The concerns and hesitation that Diane and Melanie may have had about attaching an unknown actor in this role disappeared after viewing it. They were not only convinced that I could make the script into something compelling to watch, but had also come to believe that Neil was the right person for the role. Fishbowl Films was willing to move forward with the dates and invest in the film immediately.

Literally days before we began production, Diane and Melanie signed on as producers. At last, we had a budget that we could work with. Ultimately, we raised $40,000. With hard work and a strong belief in what we were doing, my team managed to make a film that had production values you'd expect in a film with a much higher budget.

PRE-PRODUCTION

In addition to casting Neil Hopkins, I auditioned a number of actresses for the role of Jackson's girlfriend Laurie. I was fortunate that Neil came to the auditions so he could test the scenes with them. Most of the scenes with Jackson's girlfriend involved Jackson recording her on his cell phone camera, which required the actress to play the scenes directly to the camera. This provided the perfect opportunity to both audition these women and record them simultaneously.

Casting the Film

Auditions are extremely difficult for both the actor and the director. It's near impossible to determine if the person is right for the role when you only get a few minutes, and in some cases a few seconds, to consider the actor and his or her interpretation of the character. If you have the time, I encourage you to spend five to ten minutes with the actor. Run through the scene, or scenes, at least twice. That way you will have an opportunity to make suggestions and see how it affects his or her performance the second time around. Even if actors give you a performance that you like in their first attempt, it is worth throwing a random adjustment at them to see how they adapt to it.

If you can communicate easily with an actor, and they in turn can translate your direction into behavior that advances the story you're trying to tell, you're in real good shape. By giving some direction in auditions, you can quickly ascertain your ability to communicate with the actor. That's important. If actors are late to auditions, if they show up significantly unprepared, if they exhibit attitudes—negative attitudes outside of the state of mind of their characters—this conduct may be indicative of how pleasant, or how unpleasant, your professional working relationship with them will be in the future.

I've been told that my auditions run long, but I don't see the harm in that. These are the people who are going to bring your characters to life on screen. In many ways, the actors hold the key to the film's success. Spend the time to cast the film properly; you'll thank yourself for it when you're in the editing room.

I also think it's important to film the auditions, whether the actors are performing to the camera or not. Sometimes actors read better on film than they do in person. When it comes down to it, this isn't theatre, this is cinema, and the actor's performance must be right for the screen. You can certainly get a sense of whether an actor is adequate or not for a role in person, but you're not looking for adequate, you're looking for a spark of magic, magic that can only be captured through a lens and projected out onto a screen.

In the case of the *Detour* auditions, I narrowed it down to two actresses for the role of Laurie. I was leaning one way, only to completely reverse my opinion when I reviewed the two auditions later that evening on video. It's the performance on screen that matters. I auditioned Brea Grant, an up-and-coming actress who had just completed a successful run on the NBC show *Heroes*, and she knocked the audition out of the park. There were subtleties in her performance that I had not fully detected during the audition but that I noticed later on the video.

The delineations of the character that Brea exhibited in her audition were right on the money. She also had tangible chemistry with Neil and was able to take my suggestions and run with them. I hired her the next day.

Rehearsing

This was a SAG low-budget production, which meant we were only required to pay the actors $100 a day. Basically, they were doing the film because they wanted to. As I mentioned earlier, pitch actors on the role, and if they see themselves in the part, they usually have to do it—pay or no pay. Actors want to work, and they want to do good work, because good work leads to more work.

I scheduled one day of rehearsal for the scenes with Neil and Brea. I had been talking through the script with Neil for a couple of months, but the script was new to Brea, and once I cast her in the part, the scenes became new to Neil. Before, Laurie was just a name on a page, but now she was inhabited by a living, breathing person who brought pieces of herself to the part. Neil had to get to know her, and vice versa.

Budget often determines whether or not there will be rehearsals; it can get expensive since these are considered work days for actors and you're required to pay them. Actors' schedules can also be exceedingly tight, so they may not have much time outside the shoot dates to dedicate to rehearsal. Rehearsals typically take place in the days directly prior to the shoot. I recommend that you fight for a week of rehearsal, but if you can only get one day, take it.

Some directors think rehearsing ruins the spontaneity of the performance. Some think a scene can never be over-rehearsed. My opinion resides somewhere between these two points of view. I like to rehearse the scenes, but I don't want the actors to act, or at least not much. What I mean by that is, I think rehearsals are important in the same way that dribbling drills in a soccer practice are beneficial to the team come the game on Sunday. I like the actors to exercise their muscles in the same way that athletes do. If you're the coach of a sports team, you don't want your athletes to wear themselves out before the big game. Practices build up the strength of the players so that they'll be at their top level of performance when they need to be. Practices are typically divided into sections of drills and routines, which are meant to focus on different skills—skills that when combined later on game day exhibit the pinnacle of the player's potential.

The first thing you must do in rehearsal, and the most important thing to do in rehearsal, is a read-through of the script. The key to acting is listening, and the more the actor is allowed to simply listen to the dialogue spoken by the actor(s) in the scenes, the better his or her performance will be.

This should be a read-through of the entire script with the director and the actors, no one else. I ask the actors to read through the script once, uninterrupted and without any acting. Then I have them read it once again. As they read through it a second time, I tell the actors to stop the reading if they have a question to ask or a point to make. Then we talk about it.

Discussing the script in this fashion is crucial; actors are intrinsic storytellers just like you, and discussions about motivations are good to delve into while going over the script. Your cast might want to know why a character does certain things, the dynamics between characters, the backstory of these relationships, how these backstories contribute to the obstacles standing in the way of the character getting what he or she wants. There is a slight danger of over-intellectualizing the story, but I feel that there is room for some analysis of the themes and the vision that you're going after as a director in this initial stage of the rehearsal process. Over-intellectualizing is more of a problem on set, when it's time to act, time to play objectives and let a character's behavior reveal the subtext. The set is not the place for a profound exploration of the script, since it is often unhelpful for the actor to think too cerebrally about the scene.

TIP ▶ PRE-PRODUCTION IS THE TIME FOR QUESTIONS.

Actors will always have questions and they will always have suggestions, and both are very good things and necessary parts of their jobs. However, once production begins, you will find that you do not have nearly as much time as you thought you would have to do everything that you need to do. Too many questions on set can be detrimental to the process and slow the momentum of the schedule.

While you're shooting, you will not only be fielding questions from the actors, but also addressing the plethora of miscellaneous questions from the heads of all the creative departments. You will not have time to answer everyone's question (unless you've padded the schedule). If you try to, you will undoubtedly seem like you're being short with people or not devoting much attention to their needs—or as much as they would like or expect you to. Questions and input from your collaborators should be encouraged, just preferably not during the shooting. There's too much to do, too many questions to answer, as many questions as there are seconds in a day. You should prepare at least ten answers to every possible question you could think of someone asking on the set.

After I finished reading through the script with Neil and Brea and addressed any issues or concerns they may have had, I began to physically rehearse their scenes with them. Before I started, I told them I did not want them to put any emotions into the performances, that I wanted them to just get a feeling for the lines and experiment with blocking. In my mind, I already had a specific way that I wanted to block the actors, but it is unwise to tell them before the get-go where it is that you want them to be at every second in the scene. Actors will always have input on where their characters should move, or not move. Some of their input will work, and some of it will not.

My point is, if you instruct your actors where to go in the first rehearsal, and these instructions are to be the same on the day of the shoot, you're setting yourself up to fail. I say that because actors will most always have feedback or suggestions regarding blocking, so if on the first day of rehearsal they disagree with your master blocking, what do you do then? I suppose you can say to your actor, *I'm the director, and you must do what I say when I say it,* but that never goes over very well, especially if you reach the point when the actor is more valuable of a commodity than the director.

As for blocking the actors in rehearsal, I usually say something like: "I'd like the scene to start over here [*indicating an area of the rehearsal space*], and then somewhere around the end of the scene, let's see if we can try to end up over here? Let's run it a few times and see how that feels. Is that okay?"

This is scene direction at its most general. Later, I may have other things to add that will impact the movement in the scene. For example, in one scene Laurie steps into her garden, sees that it has been ravaged by animals, and bends down to inspect the destruction. Basically, by suggesting bookends of where on the set you would like the scene to start and where you would like it to end, you are giving freedom to the actors to find their own way through the scene. By giving Brea her beginning and end points, I allowed her room to discover the middle of the scene on her own. While she was discovering it, I would make subtle suggestions as to where I thought her character would be in specific beats, and she was very receptive to the input—we were organically working through the scene together.

After you've roughly blocked the scenes and the actors have their bearings, I recommend running the scenes with them over and over and over without saying a word. Just like the drills a coach has his athletes run, over and over and over. You should try to run them without giving any direction. You can say "good," but don't say "great" or "excellent," or worse, "perfect." If the scene were perfect, you wouldn't have to run it anymore, would you? The only time you should ever say "that's perfect!" is when you're on set, and you're shooting, and it's the last take of the last shot in the scene you are filming. Otherwise, you're bullshitting your actors and they will know you are bullshitting them. If you tell them it's perfect and then immediately ask for another take, the actors are quickly going to learn to not trust you.

Actors must be given room to experiment. This is how they find their characters. Too much specific direction by the director at this early stage will stymie actors and negatively affect their performances. An actor may feel that the director doesn't trust him, or a more experienced actor may begin to doubt the director's self-confidence. Micromanaging a scene early on may be indicative of some kind of burgeoning insecurity, which in turn may lead the actor to distrust the director and potentially do the opposite of what he asks.

Trust is the most important thing to establish between actor and director. Without trust, the working relationship between actor and director will rapidly disintegrate.

Some actors like to make *large* choices in rehearsal, choices that may seem over-the-top, but sometimes they make this choice as a place to start and then bring it down as they rehearse more, so that when they perform the scene in front of the camera they will have internalized much of the acting they started with and give a performance that's filled with subtlety and nuance. On the other hand, some actors make *small* choices in rehearsal, choosing to gradually find the emotion and build up to it, nurturing it, saving it, so when they are finally in front of the camera everything that they need to flesh out their characters will just pour out of them on "action."

There are countless ways an actor prepares for the moment he or she will be in front of a camera, and I guarantee you that each of these ways has the same thing in common: the performance the actor gives in the first rehearsal will not be the same as the performance in front of the rolling cameras. Therefore, you shouldn't be worried or jump to conclusions or start dispensing an overabundance of direction if you're not getting what you want in rehearsal. Give it time.

Hitchcock was famous for allegedly saying that all actors are cattle. Well, that's certainly not true anymore. You are dealing with real people in an organic, mutating art form. The story, and the elements used in telling the story, will continue to change from the first draft of the script all the way up until it is shrink-wrapped in a Blu-ray box on your shelf. It is your job to get out of its way and guide it to its greatest possible height.

SUMMARY

If you can find the money to make the film you visualize, while actually paying your friends to work, that's great! However, the more money you attract, the more you have to be willing to compromise, and often it's you who are asked to make the sacrifices. It's understandable that investors want to avoid too much risk, but ask yourself how much you are willing to put up with. Sometimes the changes you have to make can lead to valuable insights. Other times the money may not seem worth it. Sit down with yourself and some trusted advisors to come up with an honest answer. In the end, the film might be a little rough around the edges, but it will be *your* film.

CHAPTER FIVE

PRODUCTION

We started shooting in May of 2010, starting with the aboveground scenes. Those first three days of shooting went smoothly, though they were unquestionably taxing. One thing you must grapple with, if you set a date and stick to it no matter what, is that you'll end up doing a lot of things yourself. I was the writer, I was the director, but I was also going to the mall with actors and buying them their wardrobes. I was also driving the U-Haul truck and picking up equipment, and I was arranging plants in a backyard garden in the name of production design.

But it was invigorating. It brought me back to AFI, where they encouraged each of their students to do everything. If you weren't directing, you were holding the boom on your classmate's project. AFI taught me humility, and DIY ethics—which is ironic, if you think about it, since the school is in many ways a mirror image of the Hollywood system. **However, it showed me that in any industry and in any point in a career, if you want something done right, you should always be able to rely on yourself.**

And that AFI experience came in enormously handy in this instance. Something I learned early on was whether you're directing a film on a zero budget, or on a budget with nine zeroes, you wake up fifteen minutes early and pick up a box of donuts on the way to set. You have no idea how far that seemingly little gesture will go with the crew. Even if someone doesn't eat donuts, or only eats gluten-free vegan donuts (there is one vegan on every set, if not two, so be prepared, Craft Services and Catering departments), it still shows that you care.

Working on a movie set can be backbreaking work, and it's often work for very little money, so never take your crew for granted. If people enjoy the work and want to be there with you, that unambiguous passion will show through to the screen.

STAY CALM AND KEEP DELETING

As seemingly smooth as those first three days went, we hit the first big bump just as we were preparing to shoot one of the most important scenes of the film, which also happened to be a revealing emotional moment for Brea's character. It was a flashback in which Jackson finds Laurie in the bathroom, straddling the toilet after having just endured a late-term miscarriage. Blood (the fake kind) was all over the place, on Brea's legs, on her satin nightgown, on the floor, on the bottoms of Neil's shoes. Brea was weeping; Neil was wincing. I wanted to shoot everything in one shot, a steadicam shot, of course, but without an actual steadicam because that would have been way too expensive. So Rob held the camera in his hands and absorbed as much shock through his knees as he could. It took hours and hours to light and an extremely long time to rehearse the 2½ minute shot. I didn't let anyone talk, since this was a scene in which the actors were extremely vulnerable and exposed—until Neil started cracking jokes about the horrific sight his character was walking into: "Hi honey, I'm home...omigod did you have a miscarriage again?!"

This diversion turned out to be good, considering an essential wire broke that connected the RED camera to an external hard drive. This wire was vital to offloading footage in order to free up space on the camera's memory card, which only had enough space for one take of one of the most complex shots in the film. Since RED cameras are only compatible with RED accessories, this was a part that we could not get at Radio Shack, and considering it was 10:45 PM on a Sunday evening, we were out of luck. So I'm glad Neil broke the ice, because this scene was getting on everyone's nerves. By the time we got around to shooting it, we only had another 30 minutes with the actors before we had to let them go for the night.

Yes, this supremely sucked. However, it would have sucked a lot more if we only had enough film in the camera's magazine for one take. At least with a digital camera we had the ability to shoot a take, and if we didn't like it, we could delete the file, free up room, and try it all over again, stopping when we finally got a shot we liked. What a relief to be able to shoot the scene, review it on a screen the size of a business card to see if it passed muster, and then decide whether or not to **erase the entire shot** and try it again in an attempt that may or may not be better than the last.

Heartburn. Mucho heartburn.

We ended up shooting the scene eight times, and we were pleased enough with the last take to call it a night and let the actors go with about 30 seconds to spare before we would go into overtime according to SAG regulations. The shot, really, turned out to be amazing. However, we eventually cut the scene from the film—a decision that had nothing to do with the quality of the shot, but everything to do with story. After various test screenings, we realized that the flashback-to-miscarriage storyline was going over people's heads and determined that it wasn't absolutely necessary to the plot. So we hacked it.

It is important to remember that there are no sacred cows in this profession, despite the anguish my DP suffered when I told him his favorite and most labored-over shot was summarily tossed onto the cutting room floor.

It's important to love your work, your script, your shots, your technique, but never *fall in love* with any of it. The moment you do, you've abandoned objectivity, and it's objectivity that will ultimately allow your craft to thrive and affect a broader audience in the same way that it affects you.

CARS, MUD, AND GOOD FORTUNE

My partnership with Diane and Melanie of Fishbowl Films turned out to be nothing short of serendipitous. After we completed the above-ground material, we began preparing to shoot the car stuff, which basically consisted of the other 85% of the film. We spent the next month prepping this material and set a date in mid-July to begin production. Melanie just happened to know precisely the right people we were looking for to get help.

In addition to Jackson, the other main character of the film is the car. Jackson spends the longest three days of his life inside this vehicle, and risks life and limb to finally escape it. The car is a character, and much like the volleyball "Wilson" was in *Cast Away*, this inanimate object becomes personified as the film progresses.

The Importance of Cultivating Connections

Melanie was a lifelong friend of Ted Moser, owner of the Picture Car Warehouse. PCW is the place where, if you need a car for a movie and you need it rigged to be shot from inside, you go to get it. They rigged the van for *Little Miss Sunshine*. Ted found the exact mid-90's Jeep Cherokee that I was looking for and had his team of mechanics cut the car up to my exact specifications: the doors, the roof, the windshield, the dash, the floor, and the sunroof were all removable. We could shoot an angle through the air conditioning vent if we wanted, and you know what, we did!

We also needed mud, an obscene amount of mud, in various states of ooziness. If the protagonists were Jackson and, by extension, his car, the physical antagonist was the mud that surrounded and encroached on them. Ted just happened to ask us: "Do you have a practical effects guy?" Until that point, I was prepared to be the practical effects guy, just as I had been the truck driver a week earlier, dousing the car with mud after I called action. I was prepared to do everything, but gradually I realized that I didn't have to.

It was actually happening! I had pulled the train out of the station, and there were actually people who were hopping on board along with me and taking the ride.

Ted asked his buddy Bob Williams for a favor; specifically, he asked him to help us out with our film. Bob, in addition to being Ted's friend, was a bona fide legend in the effects business. He built the original Terminator robot in James Cameron's *Terminator*. He was also the most fearless man I'd ever met. (Later in the production, he nearly sliced his finger off constructing the practical cracking sunroof in the ceiling of the car, but didn't even blink as he wrapped the wound in gaffer's tape and continued working.) And now this guy was going to be making mud for my film. It was pretty unbelievable.

Melanie also brought on Jamison Goei, the visual effects supervisor on *Twilight*, whom she met while working at Neo Art & Logic. She not only persuaded Jamison to do the VFX for the film, but she also somehow convinced him to invest money in the project. Amazing, really. She also recruited Henning Lohner, the composer for *The Ring* and *The Ring Two*, and Kirk Morri, editor of *Insidious* and *The Conjuring*, to join the cause later in post-production.

It was as if Melanie were cashing in all her favors for this very project, and if that was indeed the case, I'm really glad she did!

There is a reason why you develop connections over the years of paying your dues in this town, and the reason is that one day you will call upon these connections for support, and this was a terrific example of that process at work. It also just happened to be the perfect project for Melanie and all her colleagues, and I think she was well aware of that when she decided to get involved. It may have taken three years to get this project to this point, but sometimes it just takes time for an idea to end up in the right home and in the hands of the most caring parents.

In addition to bringing such wonderful talent into the project, Fishbowl Films was able to match our current funds. In a matter of days, they had doubled our budget, and well exceeded what we'd originally planned for the project in terms of talent, resources and labor.

TIP ▶ TURN PROBLEMS INTO OPPORTUNITIES.

We had secured an enormously discounted deal with a sound-stage in Inglewood, near Randy's Donuts, which was good for me and my taste buds, but it was also near LAX, which was definitely not very good for sound.

Throughout the shoot, the sound of planes overhead was a frequent nuisance, but Neil and I ended up working out an effective solution when this occurred. Each time he heard a plane during a take, he would act as if it were the sound of creaking, as though the mud around the car was compressing the metal, crushing the structure of the vehicle. It worked really well; it kept Neil in the moment and we were able to replace the plane sounds with the creaking effects later in the sound design phase.

Working with Actors, Cars, and Mud

Picture Car Warehouse delivered the car, along with a Bobcat bulldozer they lent us. While we prepped the car and my production designer dressed the set, Melanie assigned another art director friend of hers to the task of building the tunnel portion of the set. This tunnel was to be suspended above the car as Jackson ascends through the mud to make his harrowing escape in the third act of the film. My production designer, meanwhile, set about acquiring endless amounts of actual dirt.

We hadn't even begun to shoot the car stuff and the set was slowly, but surely, transforming into the filthiest anyone had ever stepped foot on. This was most definitely a good sign, in my opinion.

Once the art department finished dressing the car and the mechanics showed us how to disassemble it, I scheduled one full day of rehearsal with just myself and Neil on a closed set. Then there was another half day for a technical rehearsal, which I required Neil and all heads of departments to attend as I blocked out every scene in the script that involved the car.

Neil and I had scoured the script several times together, so much of the thematic elements and motivation for Jackson's character had been touched on beforehand. This is absolutely key. Since you're paying actors for these rehearsal days, and the run of the entire set doesn't come cheap, you're required to be efficient.

Your goal in the physical rehearsal on the set is to block everything you can, down to the most minimal of movements. This way, you avoid wasting time blocking and re-blocking while the set is lit on a shoot day and the entire crew is standing around, on the clock, waiting for you to finish up.

As I stated earlier, don't concern yourself too much with the emotions of the scenes, especially in a rehearsal on the actual set. Concern yourself with the technical aspects of where your actor is physically going to be during each beat of every scene. This will most likely be the actor's first time on set, and the set itself (if it's designed properly) will inform much of his emotion. Let the actor take it all in. As he explores the set physically, do not ask him to act; that will distract him from absorbing his surroundings.

An actor is trained to understand his given circumstances—along with his character's backstory and objectives in the scene—and reconfigure them into actionable behavior; but he needs time to absorb everything first, including his first encounter with the set. If you've done your homework, giving the actor what he requires to build his character properly, and the actor reciprocates, dedicating one hundred percent of his mind and body to the part, when you call action on the day, the emotion will come on its own.

Directors cannot force emotion; if they try, it's nine times out of ten a surefire way of extinguishing any emotion that is there brewing under the surface or that will need to be there as the scene progresses.

The next day was the first official day of shooting on the soundstage, technically the fourth day of the shoot as a whole, even though the first three days happened approximately one month prior. As I stated, the first half of the day was to be dedicated to tech rehearsal, then afterwards we would commence with principle photography inside the car. I gathered the necessary eyes around the vehicle, and I ran through every scene in the car and made sure everyone saw where Neil was going to be at every beat of every sequence.

This didn't mean, of course, that Neil and I couldn't change up some of the blocking if an idea came to us during the shoot. You should always keep an open mind to fresh ideas, but you must have a detailed roadmap drawn out before you embark on the journey.

By putting in the work beforehand, you force yourself to think about what the scene is really about, what it means thematically, and how it advances the story. Based upon your answers to those questions, you then make certain visual decisions that hopefully illuminate those answers properly within the dramatic framework of the film. You cannot change up the blocking, lighting, or camera angle very easily if you don't know what the scene is actually about; however, if you've already answered those questions and are prepared to execute your vision of them, it's very easy to change things at the last minute.

We didn't go through much of the dialogue during this tech rehearsal; we simply walked through the movements in a perfunctory fashion. I instructed Neil to not act and just treat this as technically as possible. However, if you're dealing with scenes with more than one actor, and there's dialogue, I do recommend running lines during the tech. No acting whatsoever, but any opportunity for the actors to deliver their lines to one another and listen to each other's words is an opportunity you should take full advantage of.

After we completed the tech—and by completed I mean everything inside the car (the tunnel set was still being built and unavailable)—the sound recordist Steve Nelson took me aside and thanked me. He told me that it was extremely helpful, and that "so many directors I've worked with don't do this...and they have no idea how much time it would save if they did."

That was very nice of Steve, and I appreciated the comment. Ultimately, though, he appreciated it more, because he now knew exactly where he would place his mics ahead of time. Following this run-through, I gathered the crew around a television and played the test footage of the opening scene that we had shot months ago. The plan was to execute the real opening scene in a similar style, and to get everyone working on the film excited about what they were about to shoot. It seemed to work well and helped focus everyone's efforts to executing the task at hand.

We couldn't have been more prepared, and everyone involved couldn't seem any more on the same page. Then we started shooting.

THE FIRST DAY "UNDERGROUND"

It's the first shot of the day, the beginning of the very first take, and Neil climbs into the front seat of the car...then immediately whacks the back of his head on the edge of the lens. An extremely sharp piece of metal connected with a particularly painful part of the head: the boney area behind the ear. Perhaps Neil misjudged the space; we hadn't done a rehearsal with the actual camera and the car was cramped.

Neil yelped. I swear I thought he was joking—there's no way we could've had a problem this soon. Surely my luck couldn't possibly be this bad. But it was no joke, and he was in a lot of pain. It had taken an extremely long time to set this shot up. Rob had hung the camera through the sunroof into the car, securing it by a series of ratchet-straps that doubled as pullies, so he could take a 360 degree shot. We had to get it before lunch or we'd be starting off already behind, which is never the way you want to start things off in production. Neil, though he was seeing stars and visibly distressed, wanted to push through the pain and finish the shot. It didn't help that besides being a complex shot, it required numerous takes. We finally got it on the ninth take and then we broke for lunch.

TIP ▶ SHOOTING.

If at all logistically possible, make sure you and your first AD schedule the easiest shots for the first day. It always takes a good day or two for a cast and crew, no matter how expert they are in their craft, to get the production up to its most efficient speed.

We ended up getting the shot, and for me, it suited the state of Neil's character, who was supposed to be feeling a bit lightheaded and disoriented after waking up from a serious accident. It's not a method of acting I can recommend to anyone, but it sure felt real, and that read on camera. Neil was still in a good deal of pain throughout lunch and my producer Carrie and I insisted that he get a checkup at a hospital. I was hoping he would shake it off and the pain would subside, but it wouldn't, and he was worried. Even if the pain suddenly went away, it was clear that he would still be worried about it, and therefore would not have been able to act *in-the-moment*. There is no doubt in my mind that if we had continued that it would have adversely affected his performance. I had Carrie, whom he knew fairly well, personally drive him to the hospital.

In the meantime, we shot as many inserts as we could without him. We had no other actors to shoot, but this film was all about the details of this man in this car, so I used my hands and arms as doubles for Neil's. Believe it or not, this was something that I had done before in my film *Shadowbox*. Neil and I have strikingly similar limbs. I wish we shared similarly handsome looks, but that's a topic that's best explored in another book, or to a psychiatrist. I was prepared to lose the entire rest of the day, as I was excruciatingly aware of how long ER waits can be in Los Angeles. Luckily, Neil was back on set in just over two hours boasting a clean bill of health. He was still in some pain, but his mind was put at ease. He had become noticeably revitalized, which was the most important thing. The rest of the day was slow, and the incident put us behind the next day, but we were back on track.

Just when you think the stress of the day is finally over and you are about to relax, you realize the day's not over and relaxation is a utopian ideal that is simply unattainable in this line of business. Though we had procured a great soundstage for a killer price, it was in Inglewood. I live approximately an hour away from there, so I had to factor a two-hour commute into my day, on top of the twelve-hour workday. We rarely went over the twelve. In the world of independent filmmaking, typically the hours are awful, making twelve-hour days seem like banker's hours, but I strongly believe that no matter how intimidating your schedule may seem, that you keep your hours regular. Otherwise, you are putting your cast and crew at risk, forcing them to come face to face with interminable exhaustion.

On the first day of the shoot at this soundstage, not only did our lead actor suffer an injury, I got into a three-car accident on my way home from the set. It wasn't my fault: car one hit car two, which then rear-ended car three. I was car three. It was my first car accident, if you can believe it. I already have my fair share of neck issues, so the accident didn't help any, but it wasn't serious, thank goodness. I was hoping that now all the bad luck was out of the way.

ONWARD AND AWAY!

The rest of the week, we played catch-up. We didn't quite catch up completely, but we managed not to fall behind any more than we already were. Neil, meanwhile, managed *not* to kill himself—though he came close. In addition to the head injury that first day, he chipped a tooth later in the week, cut his finger on some broken glass and inhaled an ample amount of dirt. The only thing that I could assure him with any degree of certainty was that he was going to inhale a lot more dirt in the days to come.

The Actor

To say Neil was a trooper is an understatement. He's my friggin' hero. He was completely professional, while risking life and limb each day—willingly, I might add. Well, okay, maybe he wasn't really risking his life, but he wholeheartedly dedicated himself to selling the reality of the film to the audience, specifically the horror of his character's predicament. He *was* Jackson Alder, flesh and blood, and he immersed himself in the darkness that was required of the character.

In my film *Shadowbox*, there was an interrogation scene in which Neil was chained to the floor with a burlap sack over his head. In the story, he and other prisoners had been chained up like this for close to twenty-four hours. When Neil arrived on set, while we were lighting the first shot, he went to wardrobe, got his burlap sack, put it over his head, and had me chain his hands together and lock him in a dark room. This was a complex shot, so it took close to four hours to set up, which meant Neil was locked in that room for four hours, concentrating, putting himself into the shoes of his character. When it came time to shoot, he asked to be physically led out and sat in his place; he didn't want to break that feeling of being imprisoned against his will. The first time the burlap sack came off his head that day was when the actor playing the interrogator in the film, Lance Guest, yanked it off when the cameras were rolling.

Neil was committed, and it showed on screen. Kelly Carlson, who most know from the show *Nip/Tuck*, played one of the other prisoners chained to the ground in the scene, and her approach differed completely from Neil's. During the four hours, Kelly sat in her car in the parking lot talking on her cell phone. This is by no means an indictment of Kelly or her methods, because when she was called to set and sat in front of the camera, she instantly transformed into the character. Her strong emotions flooded out as the sack was pulled off her head and she stared into the pitiless eyes of the interrogator.

Kelly aced it. She had spent years working in television, and in television there's very little time, if any time at all, for rehearsal. Therefore, she was used to snapping into character quicker than the director can say "action." Neil adopted more of a *method* approach. He took advantage of his time to tap into his character, to physically experience the disorientation and commit it to memory, so when the cameras rolled he could recall his experience, along with the feelings it conjured, and apply it to the scene as he locked horns with the interrogator.

Actors embrace a variety of approaches to their craft, and no one approach is better than another; you must pay attention to how each individual actor likes to work and adapt.

The Tunnel

The next couple of weeks went as planned, for the most part. The shooting experience was really inspiring, and rare. When the make-up artist wasn't painting Neil's face, she was running props to the set. When our soundman wasn't recording sound, he was screwing the doors on and off the car. We weren't forcing anybody to do anything outside his or her wheelhouse—they all wanted to be there and to do exactly what they were doing.

They wanted to do it because they believed in the film and they believed in the people bringing the film to life.

From my experience making movies, and from listening and observing the experiences of others who make movies, the ultra-supportive production experience of *Detour* was extremely uncommon. And I knew it and made sure to relish every second of it, because I thought I might never experience this kind of set again in my career.

The production ran into the most difficulty when The Tunnel finally arrived on set. We had been unable to run a technical rehearsal for the tunnel sequences since we didn't have the actual tunnel prior to principal photography on the stage. This was disconcerting because these sequences comprised about the last ten to fifteen minutes of the film. Even though this portion of the movie only existed as a handful of pages in script form, I intended it to be a major sequence on screen, ostensibly an action sequence, with numerous set-ups.

A few days before we completed the interior car scenes, the tunnel structure was delivered. Upon first glance, it looked really cool, and I had no doubt it would be visually effective—and then I touched it. The white foam had been painted brown to replicate the look of mud. What I hadn't anticipated, was that the consistency of the foam was hard as a rock. And this texture jutted out all over the place.

Aesthetically, it was great; however, to human skin it felt like miniature mountains and valleys of sandpaper. And a half-naked man was to climb up it, slide and rub against it while wearing only boxer shorts and no shoes, and carrying a forty-pound spare tire that's hanging around his neck. This was a literal spare tire, not a colloquial term for a beer belly. While I did describe this in the script, I may not have mentioned beforehand to the tunnel designer that a naked man was to be rubbing against this surface. I just assumed it was obvious from the read. The story is all about one man who digs his way out of the ground. Perhaps I assumed "foam" meant soft foam, and not hard-as-a-rock foam?

This just goes to show: assume nothing, and mention every possible thing that sticks out in your mind as an unanswered question. It is your job to protect the actor, because it is you whom the actor is putting his trust in.

In line with this notion, you should never put an actor through something that you are not willing to put yourself through. I removed my shirt, lay down in the constructed tunnel, and rubbed my bare limbs all up against it. And it really hurt.

I alerted my production designer to the issue—she had the same concern the moment she saw the tunnel—and she had her art department team pack the inside of this tunnel with fresh mud, which made it a lot easier on the skin as someone traversed through it. Another problem was that the foam that lined the tunnel's interior broke off really easily, and when it broke off, it would leave a spot of bright white. This sequence was meant to be dark, the set and the actor, swathed in darkness, but when a piece of the foam broke off, it left a spot of white that stood out like a sore thumb.

Layering actual dirt and mud over the surface was a decent remedy; it softened the surface and helped prevent the foam from breaking off. The problem was that it took forever. I would have four or five people inside this tunnel packing dirt chunks into its crevices. Since the tunnel was positioned vertically, the dirt would constantly fall off. As a result, before every set-up, we had to repack the dirt. This cost us some serious time. If the tunnel had been available for the tech rehearsal, we would have been well aware of this problem and would have been prepared to tackle it in a much more efficient and less painful manner when it came time to shoot the scenes inside of it.

We also did not allocate any money in the budget to have a foam prop tire constructed as a replacement for the actual spare tire, which Neil's character was to strap around his neck and shoulders with jumper cables as he made his way up through the ground. The spare tire was much larger than I had thought it was going to be, and also much heavier. It was just over forty pounds and I was dreading the moment that I was going to ask Neil to strap this son-of-a-bitch to his shirtless chest.

This poor guy had already been to hell and back, and it was only going to keep getting worse for him. I pulled my production designer aside and asked her to discreetly work on the tire and try to figure out a way to make it more *comfortable*. I was aware of the sheer absurdity of this situation, of making a spare tire more comfortable to wear, but it had to be done. She came up with a brilliant idea to tear portions of the blanket he used in the car as makeshift shoulder and neck pads, protecting his skin from the jumper cables, which were sure to dig into him from the weight of the tire.

I tested it out; it was wearable, but it certainly wasn't *that* comfortable on me. I lasted about five minutes with it on. Then I tested it out with Neil. I had made sure that no one mentioned the idea of creating a prop tire—I knew we couldn't afford it, but if Neil insisted we create one, we had to find a way to make it happen, period. I told him that I intended for him to wear the actual tire, precisely because it was real, precisely because it would help him in the scene. Having said all that, I was nevertheless ready for him to flat out refuse to wear it. And he would have been well within his right to.

To Neil's absolute credit, he liked the fact that he could feel the weight. It meant less acting that he was required to do; his physical reactions to the tire as he traversed the tunnel would be completely authentic, because it was real.

It was one less given circumstance that he needed to address; he would simply use the obstacle to his advantage. I salute his bravery. You can feel the weight of this contraption, and its effect on his demeanor, on the screen. That's the kind of dedication that separates the men from the boys. It was also the kind of set in which he felt safe. Everyone was looking out for everyone else, and that goes back to everyone wanting to be there in the first place. If everyone is passionate about the project, everyone will go the extra mile, and the cream of the emotion will rise to the top of the story.

Filmmaking can be a wonderfully organic process, but only if the story is provided with the right environment in which to thrive.

The Products

As artistic an environment as this set was—which was surely due to the fact that this was microbudget and there were no studio executives breathing down our necks—corporate America still wiggled its way into the process.

I write this half-jokingly, since we specifically called on product placement companies to furnish us with samples so that we could use them in the car. Point in fact, there are several key items that our main character uses that facilitate his escape, and in doing so, they take on significantly more meaning as the movie progresses. Some of these items include water bottles, a flashlight, newspapers, motor oil, "The Club" anti-theft gadget, a bag of pretzels, Jeep Cherokee, and an iPhone, to name a few. Most of these items were provided to us for free, and those that were provided were cleared, so we could legally show the brand names on camera. Melanie had a good relationship with a product placement company that provided us with boxes of chocolate-covered Flipz Pretzels, and to them I owe a wealth of gratitude. They even gave us the white chocolate kind. I kept eating the props, and then magically more bags would appear, and it kept recurring just like that. It was miraculous.

The company was not paying us to use products in the film as a sort of advertisement—their service merely allowed us to show the products on camera with full legal clearance. Still, I felt they wanted us to use more and that I was being compelled to do so. I wish I could adopt David Lynch's take on product placement (which, if you haven't seen the YouTube clip, do yourself a favor and look it up). At the 2007 AFI Dallas International Film Festival, he was asked by an enthusiastic journalist, "There seems to be a growing trend in Hollywood now where there's a lot of prominent product placement...How do you as a filmmaker feel about this growing trend?" Lynch's response was quite succinct: "Bullshit. That's how I feel. Total. Fucking. Bullshit."

Perhaps if I were a director of his stature, I might have the brass to respond similarly, since the intent of art and the intent of advertising are two diametrically opposite things. I would like to believe they are, anyway. I was asked to use a type of motor oil that was unique for the oil's color, and the color was purple. I discounted the idea since there were very few props in the car, and anything unusual about them would make them stick out even more.

The props need to blend; they're not there to be noticed for the sake of noticing them, unless there is a particular detail in a product that needs to be highlighted for the sake of story.

There was nothing in the story that beckoned for purple motor oil; therefore, to include it risked distracting the audience watching the film. An element in a film that screams product placement is never good for a story, unless it's used by way of parody, like the product placement in the *Austin Powers* movies. I hadn't been to a Chili's prior to watching Fat Bastard spout off about how much he loved his *baby-back, baby-back, baby-back ribs* in *The Spy Who Shagged Me*. Thank you very much, Fat Bastard, for enlightening my palette. Short of that, product placement can often be a slippery proposition.

Despite the efforts to convince me to use the purple motor oil, I ended up going with a standard "Motor Oil" brand motor oil. Simple. No one will ever notice, nor care that it's not an actual brand name. We applied that same treatment to a credit card that Jackson used to funnel dripping water from the sunroof into a plastic bottle and we also scratched out the "Sharpie" logo on a few markers he used inside the car.

Perhaps the most amusing product that I was encouraged to use was Emergen-C; you know, the packets of highly concentrated amounts of vitamin C, antioxidants and electrolytes delivered in the form of flavored powder mixed into a glass of water. This was also a good example of how the logic of the story dictates many of the decisions that may, on the surface, seem to fall outside the realm of story. A couple of small packets of Emergen-C on the floor of his car, or sitting benignly in the glove box as he roots through it, wouldn't really hurt anybody, right? Perhaps no one would even notice, and it would make the placement company happy. But, you see, someone always notices, and that often leads to distraction.

Nothing is perfect, and someone will always find something to criticize the film for, but part of your job is minimizing those slips and giving viewers as little to complain about as possible.

Perhaps a packet of Emergen-C would do no harm, maybe it's on camera for a half a second, and just maybe Jackson uses it. These packets are filled with nutritious vitamins. He could open one up and lap up every last antioxidant and electrolyte. It would make sense for his nutrient-deprived character to do, and it could provide him and the story a nice energy boost. However, a significant part of the story involves water; specifically, Endeara Springs Water, the fictional water bottle company whose advertising campaign Jackson Alder is in charge of in the story. He has one unopened bottle of Endeara Springs Water that must last him through his three days underground.

There is a specific arc to this prop: it starts out as a container for the spring water, and when the water is gone, Jackson refills it with dirt-water that he extracts from the mud dripping through his sunroof, and then when that water is gone, he fills the bottle up with his urine, which he's been stockpiling in the vat of his center console. If Jackson had Emergen-C packets at his disposal, he most certainly would use them in his bottle of urine to mask the putrid taste of the beverage in its natural form. Artificially flavoring his urine would be at the top of the list for uses of Emergen-C in this type of predicament, so for him not to employ the product in such a manner violated the logic of the film.

I had Melanie ask the product placement company if we could incorporate their client's product into the story in this fashion. I wish I could have seen the face of her contact when Melanie asked her this question. Heck, this is the movies, I'm sure product placement companies have fielded far worse queries regarding the use of their products. Melanie was a trooper to ask them such a question on my behalf.

Unfortunately, they would not allow us to use the product to flavor our character's pee, even if that meant alienating a niche market of individuals out there who just might use Emergen-C for that expressed purpose.

All things considered, I never encountered any major issues with product placement on this go-around. We were a no-budget film that was more worried about clearing the products we had to use in the film, rather than using products for financial reward. And Melanie handled all of this with aplomb. I was not being asked to incorporate a power drill into the story, which the company I mentioned earlier tried to coerce me to do, so I thank her very much for that.

THE SEQUENTIAL NATURE OF MUD

Because of the nature of our set—specifically that we were only in possession of a single car, which was being destroyed incrementally every day that we shot—we were obliged to shoot all of the car scenes according to the chronology in the script. Once the mud started to invade the inside of the vehicle, there was no turning back. For instance, there's a moment when Jackson attempts to open a window, and when he's finally able to open it just a crack, mud pours in, staining the beige seats and his entire outfit.

We had another shirt (we only could afford three, since Neil dragged me to Banana Republic to shop for his wardrobe), but the inside of the car was toast. We could only shoot that shot once, and we had to get it right because there was no resetting it—the mud had already made its mark.

Generally, films are not shot in sequence because it is not cost-effective to do so. Shooting in sequence is wonderful for actors, especially actors who are used to working uninterrupted on the stage, since they're able to stay in character throughout the entirety of their arcs. However, shooting in this manner is often terrible for the bottom line. For example, if several scenes that are scattered throughout a script take place in the same location, they would be scheduled to be shot in a row at the location. The production might only be able to get that location for two days. It would be too expensive to hold it for the two weeks they would need if they wanted to shoot the entire script in order.

There are plenty of reasons to not shoot a movie in chronological order, and most all of them have to do with money.

In the case of *Detour*, we didn't have a choice; we had to shoot it in sequence. And it just happened that this was optimal for Neil, as well as for myself, since we could remain focused on the development of his character and the story in the way they were meant to progress. However, we did carry the burden of knowing that we couldn't reshoot anything. And that's a significant weight to carry.

Fortunately, I had about three years to troubleshoot the script and envision how the story would be best translated to the screen, but once you're on set, things are bound to go wrong and you have no choice but to roll with it.

Editing on the Go

We were also handicapped by not being able to screen dailies in the evenings or having an editor attached to the project while in production. It's a great help to sift through the footage you shot earlier in the day. This allows you to make sure you got everything you needed to tell the story properly. It also gives you time to reflect in a darkened room with just a handful of people, unlike the stress of being on the set shooting the footage. We simply did not have the resources, or the time, to screen dailies after shoot days.

I'm not entirely sold on the necessity of watching dailies, either. While I think it's beneficial, it's also beneficial to sleep. I'm sure it's easier to work the ritual of dailies into larger budget studio films, since watching them may very well require little more than a brief stroll across the lot. But in independent filmmaking, it is often much harder to work this step into your schedule and your budget.

The potential remedy to this, which I find is far more helpful, is hiring an editor in pre-production. That way, he or she is around in production to watch the filming and the subsequent footage. Editors are in the best position to bring to your attention shots that you may have missed, or that you should get, so that the scene cuts together properly.

I've heard some contentious stories involving editors on set giving the director their opinions during the shoot, but I urge you to resist such reservations—you don't have to listen to the editor, but you should, since he is about to become your best friend (hopefully) in post-production. He is also in a position to be completely objective about story. Most likely he was not involved creatively in pre-production, so all he has is a script and what he is seeing unfold before him on set. Everything he sees, whether it is indeed on set or in dailies, is observed through his own storytelling lens, and that will shape how he puts the shots together. I'm sure countless directors have found themselves lamenting on the cutting-room couch, "Shit, I wish I had gotten that shot...." Well, if your editor was involved in production, you probably would've gotten that shot and you would be cheering rather than tearing your hair out.

One of the obvious benefits of shooting digitally is that you can instantly review your shots without having to stick them in a can and send them to a lab to be developed, which is a costly and time-consuming endeavor. I bring this up with respect to dailies because of a quintessential moment in my film that involved Jackson getting ready to climb up and out of his car through the dirt. It is a crucial moment because he could give up—he's been through a horrendous ordeal and he knows that the dirt could all collapse on him if he attempts to dig his way out. He knows that by trying to escape, he also increases his chances of dying.

We filmed Neil breaking the sunroof of the car and then starting his journey up through the dirt, and we filmed this at the very end of one of our shoot days. I thought I had gotten everything I needed to tell the story of this moment, but when I got into bed that night I felt like I may have missed something. The first thing that I did when I arrived on set the next morning was sit down with Rob, fire up the RED hard drive and skim through every shot in the scene that we filmed the previous night. Sure enough, I never shot a close-up of Neil's face after the falling dirt and glass settle and he looks through the sunroof at the dirt, his antagonist, situated before him like an old foe he's getting ready to do battle with.

I needed to see that moment of decision on Neil's face, the do-or-die expression that communicates to the audience that he's decided to try and live, that he's going to do so by digging through this dirt like a mole, and that he wasn't about to surrender and die in there. It was just a look, but it was a look that said everything, and I didn't have it.

We scheduled this shot for first thing in the morning, and then we moved on to the following scene. We missed shots on three occasions, from what I recall. Each time the problem was solved by skimming through the digital footage in the morning and shooting the shot that we needed shortly after. The ability for us to summon up any shot we wanted onto my DP's computer was crucial to our success as filmmakers, especially since we couldn't screen dailies. And we wouldn't have been able to do this if we were shooting on film.

In microbudget filmmaking, digital video is most certainly your friend.

Special Effects and Dead Birds

Once the mud began to flow, the set got dirtier and dirtier and the soundness of the car's frame became less and less reliable. Everything about the car was practical: the glass was real, so when it cracks on screen, it was really cracking during the shoot. When the roof collapses and crunches into itself, that was the actual roof.

Our special effects supervisor Bob Williams was situated on the outside of the car destroying its integrity, while Neil was inside the car reacting to it imploding in on him. Yes, it was a controlled environment, but it looks real because it was real and anything can happen at any given time, so maintaining the safety of the cast and crew was front and center in everyone's mind.

Bob was like the sage of the set, filled with wisdom and wonderful stories about working with John Frankenheimer, for instance. This man not only worked on the *Terminator* films, but also did the special effects for *The Goonies* and *The Shawshank Redemption*. The guy was kind of a legend in this town. I was flattered when he compared our set to James

Cameron's set on the first *Terminator* flick. He said it had that same feeling, the feeling of making something cool and interesting outside of Hollywood's grasp; it had that unquenchable energy. He was working special effects on the reboot of television's *Beverly Hills 90210* and he would sneak away from that job and head over to our set for the "really fun stuff" that he enjoyed doing.

It was nice to have a seasoned professional like Bob validating our filmmaking process in such a way. It meant we must have been doing something right.

We did, however, run into some trouble with our fake bird. Around the time the back seat gets completely covered in wet mud and chunks of dirt, Jackson discovers that a dead bird has fallen into the car, presumably plopping down through an ever-expanding hole in the sunroof. We could not afford a taxidermied bird, or anything that resembled a genuine winged creature. What I learned from this experience is that there's a dollar and a cent to be made in Hollywood's trafficking of replica animals. We could not rent a dead bird, since we were going to submerge it in mud, so we had to buy it if we wanted to use it. To buy one would have cost us an obscene amount of money, a number that went well into the thousands of dollars.

Well, we couldn't afford it, so our art director got the next best thing, which was more of a Christmas ornament than a facsimile of an actual bird. We were lucky that we were covering it in mud, but even that didn't work very well. It was either we showed the bird—the very fake bird—or showed a glob of mud in Neil's hand.

Since we were able to examine the footage, we noticed that it could be an issue of distraction so I attempted to try to find us a better bird at the last minute. I telephoned my neighbors, Jim and Jen, and asked them if they knew where I could locate a dead bird. Jen responded, "I just happen to have two dead birds in my freezer." Not one, but two, dead birds. If you think this is strange, remember that I live in Hollywood. It was Jim who not so long ago telephoned me to ask if I had any extra fake blood. As it happened, I did, and I lent him a bottle. Jim remarked how even though Los Angeles has its drawbacks, it's a great town for making movies.

In certain parts of Los Angeles, if you happen to need fake blood, or a dead bird, you may not have to stray farther than your next-door neighbor's house—such a request is as normal as asking a neighbor to lend you a shaker of salt.

The dead birds, although genuine and perfectly preserved, unfortunately, did not work out as well as I would have liked. They deteriorated too quickly in the muck, but we were able to reshoot the ornamental bird from a couple of better angles, angles that concealed its artificiality as best as we possibly could.

SAFETY FIRST

One of the most important shots in the film, which I had conceived of years earlier, was a shot capturing the moment that the tunnel collapses and completely buries Jackson in the muck. The concept was to suspend the camera overhead, pointing down at Jackson and shooting his face in close-up as the tunnel collapses—the dirt was to rise around him, from his feet all the way up over his head, as though it is filling rapidly with quicksand.

The mud was supposed to rise completely over his head, engulfing his face, and continue rising up toward the lens. As you might imagine, this had the potential of being a pretty dangerous shot, and there was no way we could use a stunt double since it was a close-up of the character's face. The shot could only be sold if the actor did it himself.

Watching Your Actor's Back

I had spoken with Neil earlier about what I had in mind, while I was courting him for the film, and he loved the idea. He thought it would be really effective; in fact, it gave him chills. But it's one thing to talk about it when the dirt is on paper, and it's another thing altogether when it's literally about to be poured onto your head. Even though we had broached the topic before, I felt it was my responsibility to speak with Neil again about it, to explain every detail of the shot, and make sure he was completely fine with it before we went ahead and shot it.

It's important to ask permission from your actors.

Yes, they're there to do a job, and sure they're expected to perform per the guidelines in their respective contracts, but that's beside the point. By asking permission from your actors to commit to certain actions, to convey certain emotions, to willingly make themselves vulnerable on camera, you transfer your power to them. And they appreciate that. It will show in their performances. Give them the power, because when the camera rolls, you're powerless anyway.

Give your actors the power to take the reins in the moment; that's the only way the story will be conveyed truthfully.

I ran through the nuts and bolts of the shot, and Neil was gung-ho. He wanted it to look as real as possible, and as a result was willing to be buried alive. If I had to guess, I would guess that about seventy-five percent of actors in his situation would refuse to be buried alive, but Neil fully committed to the moment. He went all in.

I think this was a result of the way I described the shot to him. He knew how effective, visually, the moment would be. Some directors may feel that the camerawork, the manner in which they're portraying the actors on screen, is the province of the director and to an extent the cinematographer—not the actors. Some directors feel it is their job to shield the actors from the mechanics of the shots to keep them from getting bogged down with the conceptual part of the filmmaking process. Some directors think that withholding such information keeps them in the moment. Some directors may feel they should keep their actors entirely right brain.

But I disagree.

Actors are smart people, and if you can appeal to their intelligence by letting them in on the visual concepts and ideas behind certain shots, they will undoubtedly be more willing to take risks for you to get the shot, or shots, that you want. Actors are actors, yes, but they're actors for a reason: they have fallen in love with movies. It is their love of the art form that compelled them to pursue the craft in the first place. They came to Hollywood to pursue a dream, just like some of you did. If you can connect to that mutual feeling without getting too bogged down in the mechanics of filming, the actor may be willing to invest more in the film—and you will inevitably pull more out of him or her.

Actors are your co-conspirators in the artistic process, and that concept should be respected and practiced regularly.

In return for their allegiance to you and your film, you must protect your actors at all costs, and they must know that you're protecting them. It is that security, that protective armor that you provide them, that will enable them to cast away their inhibitions and *go for broke* on camera, because you have their backs.

Safety Protocol: First Assistant Directors are in charge of the safety of a set; therefore, all safety issues, concerns or breaches should be addressed to and filtered through them, and only them, to other relevant people.

At the beginning of each shooting day, the First AD must hold a safety meeting with the entire crew to point out potential safety hazards. On our set, people's limbs were almost constantly submerged in dirt in a variety of states: wet, dry, chunky, slimy, rocky, sticky, scratchy, and it was almost always freezing cold. We also discovered that the dirt caused a rash to break out in some of the crew, including me; I had little red bumps peppered all down my forearms and wrists. The cortisone cream was flowing in high quantities.

I must therefore thank the movie gods that Neil, of all people, was not allergic to the stuff. I mean, it had never occurred to me to ask him if he was: "Hey Neil, do you have a free hour or two? I'd like to bring over some mud, dump it into your bathtub and have you lie in it for a little while; you know, to examine how the outside of your body, and any exposed mucus membranes, reacts to the filth." I admit that I did not even think to ask him something like this in pre-production. If I make another movie involving copious amounts of dirt, I will not forget to ask this same question of everyone involved. I recall Neil asking me what kind of dirt we would be using; I assured him not to worry, that it was organic.

After the art department attached the tunnel to the roof of the car—we had to attach it to the car for a few shots that tied the inside and outside of the car together visually—a crewmember became concerned with the structural integrity of the set. It was a valid concern, and we had to continue to take measures to stabilize it further. That much was clear. The heads of the art department and special effects were attending to it. However, a mistake was made, a mistake that had nothing to do with structural integrity and everything to do with emotional integrity.

All things considered, this soundstage was a fairly small space, so Neil would often end up hanging around the vicinity of the car while art, G&E (grip & electric), or camera had the run of the set. This was fine; it was a casual environment for the most part. However, when an actor is within earshot, it is absolutely critical that the crewmembers filter their thoughts. This particular crewmember was concerned about the safety of the tunnel, expressly that the weight of it might crush the roof and possibly the actor. Even though we all knew there was still plenty of work to do, and that it was going to be secure, she began to plead her case in a panicked and public manner about how potentially unsafe the construction was. Neil was right there. He hopped into the backseat of the car and looked up into the tunnel as he listened to her.

Neil then said something to the effect of, "*This really isn't safe, is it...?*"

At that very moment, Paul Yates, our First AD, asked the crewmember to step outside with him to have a chat. He was frustrated. Paul is a director too, a very talented one, so he was thinking the same thing I was thinking: the actor is scared now. This is a big deal, which had the potential of evolving into a big problem. All the hours talking script, rehearsing scenes, technically rehearsing on the stage, blocking the scene for camera and crew, could have gone completely down the toilet if the actor suddenly felt like he was unprotected, like he couldn't *trust* me anymore.

As I've mentioned before, trust is the most important thing to an actor. Nothing trumps it. Actors have to trust the director in order to give an authentic performance, and the moment they feel like they can't trust the director anymore, or think the director doesn't have their safety in mind, it could ruin everything the director has worked so hard to establish.

It takes a long time to develop this kind of trust. Paul made it crystal clear to the crewmember that all questions and concerns that she might have regarding safety on the set must be reported to him and reported to him alone. Overall, I think this crewmember did a terrific job; she just momentarily lost her cool. The safety of the set was immediately addressed and our crew made sure the tunnel was secured properly.

The Perfect Execution

When it came time to execute the "buried alive" shot, and I use the term *execute* deliberately, the air was thick with tension. The art department constructed this contraption, which resembled a kind of medieval torture device, consisting of a three-foot portion of the tunnel set elevated about four-feet off the ground by cinder blocks. Underneath the elevated tunnel was a chair, which allowed for someone—that someone being Neil—to climb under this thing and sit inside of the tube from the waist up.

Once Neil was inside, two planks of wood were slid into a thin space that was sawed out at the bottom of the tube, one plank behind him, one plank in front of him. It looked similar to the mount on a guillotine, but instead of it locking around someone's neck, this was meant to lock around a torso. The end of each plank had a semi-circle cut out of it, so when placed together it formed a hole just big enough for Neil's waist.

The outer ends of the planks had two sets of handles drilled into them, which enabled two people to be positioned at either end (a total of four people) and pull the planks in and out of the tube when instructed.

One of the soundest investments we made was allotting money in the budget to rent a Porta-Jib, which is essentially a miniature crane about six feet in length that we affixed the camera to. We planted this sucker on our doorway dolly (you know it's a low-budget movie when the crew breaks out the doorway dolly, as opposed to the more coveted and boomable Chapman and Fisher dollies) and rolled it anywhere we wanted. Since we were dealing with a confined space, as long as we were able to remove the front, back and rear doors, roof and dashboard, we could maneuver our camera around like a snake inside that car. My DP Rob actually consulted Roto-Rooter about how they rescue kittens from pipes, because he knew they used a camera to stick down the pipes to guide them to the cats. We did not use the same type of camera they used, but we were attempting a similar feel, a look that involved a lot of movement but at the same time felt claustrophobic.

Rob extended the jib as high as it could go and suspended the camera over the tube, dipping it into the top of the tunnel. Several ladders were positioned around the outside of the tube so that everybody with free hands could dump dirt onto Neil's head. Once everything was ready to go, Neil crouched down, ducked underneath the bottom of the tube and sat down on the stool. His torso was fully enclosed within the tunnel.

As he settled into this chamber, I instructed the crewmembers manning the planks to insert them into the tube and clamp them around Neil's waist. Meanwhile, I was sitting behind my HD monitor. I think I was the only one sitting there at video village, since this shot took everyone to perform it properly. I did feel a little bad about this, like I was holed away in my ivory tower while everyone else did my dirty work. The whole ordeal did have a specter of public execution about it.

The plan was to first fill the tunnel with dirt, from the top of the planks up to Neil's shoulders, so only his neck and head were exposed. The camera would then be pointed down, its lens framing Neil's face in close-up. When I called *action*, the folks hovering on the ladders were going to pour dirt down along the sides of the tunnel. As the tunnel accumulated more and more dirt, the dirt would rise over Neil's head, burying him completely from his bellybutton to over the top of his head, and ascend right up to the glass of the lens, shrouding the frame in darkness. As soon as the frame went dark, I would call *cut*, and the four people manning the planks would grip their handles and pull their respective pieces of wood. The vat of dirt would empty to the ground at the base of Neil's feet. Neil would be able to breathe again after holding his breath for about fifteen seconds.

It all seemed simple enough.

When we were ready to shoot, we locked Neil into this apparatus and shoveled dirt around the sides of him, building it up to the top of his chest. We positioned the camera and waited until everyone situated themselves on the tops of the ladders, armed with buckets of dirt to pour into the tunnel. They were to stagger the pouring so the deluge would seem continuous on camera.

When I called *action*, the pouring began....

However, since we couldn't really do a rehearsal for this—due to time constraints and the level of manpower required—some of the crewmembers on the ladders bumped into Rob's camera as they frenetically tossed their dirt, knocking the frame away from Neil's face. There was nothing I could do. Everything was in motion and his head was just about to be covered. Rob did the best he could to realign the camera, but I knew the shot was ruined.

I called *cut*, and then I shouted the order "Pull!" so that the people manning the wooden planks pulled their pieces out and released the dirt that was smothering Neil.

I yelled it, and nothing happened, at least from what I could tell from my monitor screen. I yelled it again, still nothing.

I started to panic a bit.

I stood up and yelled it as loud as I could, and I saw that the plank people could hear me, but that they were struggling to pull the wood out. It wasn't budging. The contraption, theoretically and mechanically, made perfect sense. However, we hadn't taken into consideration how much the dirt would weigh after it was all piled up and condensed in such a manner within this tube. We just figured that four muscular people would naturally have enough strength to pull these planks out, no matter what the circumstances, and that everything would be fine. Apparently, these assumptions had been put to the test.

After the third try, the plank people managed to yank the boards out and release the dirt, but the fright remained in their eyes.

We did have a failsafe, though. If for some reason the planks got stuck, Paul would topple one entire side of the tunnel, which was only held together by a single screw, and Neil would be instantly released. We also gave Neil a gesture to make with his leg if he felt like he was in trouble, which we would recognize and promptly rip the tube open. This was a last resort, because ripping the tunnel open in this way would result in a massive amount of time to reset the shot. The failsafe was not to be enacted unless absolutely necessary.

When the dirt was released, Neil stumbled out of the device like the village drunkard, coughing and dry heaving into a corner of the soundstage. It was rough—for Neil and for everyone involved with carrying out the shot. After I let him catch his breath and drink a bottle of water, Neil approached me and asked the dreaded question every director doesn't want to answer in a situation such as this: "Did we get the shot?"

I knew that, due to the technical mishap involving the camera getting knocked about, we did not have the shot. But, the last thing I wanted to do was tell him that and then insist that he go through this torture all over again. I hesitated when he asked me that question, and it was my hesitation that answered the question before my words could.

"We didn't get it, did we?" Neil said.

I apologized and told him about the camera issue, and said that he didn't have to do it again if he didn't want to, but it would be great to get it perfect. Neil was in bad shape, and I wouldn't have faulted him for not wanting to do it again.

He said to me, "I did it once, I can do it again. This is an important shot and I want it to be perfect."

Wow! I was impressed by his fortitude, and not only that, I was honored that he felt so strongly about this film and had so much trust in me that he would endure more torture to make the film the best it could be.

That right there is the kind of character that any director hopes his actors exhibit on a project. It was exemplary, and I was damn lucky to have someone like Neil sitting next to me in the driver's seat of this show. It only took one more take to get the shot, and we nailed it.

SUMMARY

Although I like to think that I am such a great director that things will always go right, a smooth production is not the result of luck or one person. It takes a great deal of collaboration and preparation to keep to a budget and schedule and make the film that you have in your head. And no matter how prepared you may be, there will always be problems to solve and ordeals that you did not anticipate. As the director, though, you are the person that sets the tone. If your actors or crew don't see your enthusiasm or believe that they can rely on you, they won't be willing to make the strong commitment that you need. No matter how great a director you may be, nothing will work if you don't have your people supporting you too.

CHAPTER SIX

POST-PRODUCTION

As a writer, I really appreciate and understand the need for a good editor and the importance of dedicating a comfortable chunk of time in post-production to complete the cutting of the film.

Filmmaking is an organic process: the film is a wild animal that you're trying to domesticate by taking it out of the page and caging it onto the screen. **The idea dies many deaths: first when it is committed to paper; then when it is filmed; then once again when it is edited.** I believe it was Bresson who used this metaphor. Each step is, in itself, a rewrite. The editing process, in many ways, is the final rewrite of the film. And it could make or break it before the light of the projector brings the idea back to life again.

As a director, I have a firm vision of what I think the final edited cut will look like. However, I think it is also crucial to have an editor other than yourself bring his or her take on the project. You do not have to agree with it, but it will undoubtedly make you think about your film in different ways, which often leads to wonderful new ideas that you had not thought of before. This isn't because you're not capable of thinking up these new ideas, but rather because your mind has been filled up with production. You haven't been allowed enough time to separate yourself from the project and restart your brain.

The original idea, the seedling of your project, has evolved. This fundamental change becomes most apparent in the editing room, and a good editor will quickly become your confidante as he or she helps you psychologically cope with the change and facilitate its progress.

THE FIRST CUTS

After we wrapped production, I had two weeks to rest and try hard not to think about the film. And as I was doing this, Kirk was just beginning his editor's cut. It is really tough to be knee-deep in the process and then relinquish control in the middle of it, even if it's only for a week or two. But it is a necessary part of the process and should be thought of as therapeutic. It is around this time that I begin to undergo an onslaught of nightmares that result in me jolting up in bed in the middle of the night and barking orders at imaginary crewmembers around my room. My wife can't keep track of how many times she has awoken to find me sitting up in bed *sleep-directing*, and I sometimes even nudge her awake and frantically ask her, "Did we get the shot? Did we get the shot?! Please tell me we got the shot!"

She is more than used to it by now, and she replies, "Yes, you did. Go back to sleep now." This usually placates me and I fall right back to sleep, like it never happened. It's like the production has infected me with some kind of feverish virus that I can't possibly shake until I'm back in control in the editing room. I keep a director's bullhorn next to my bed, a souvenir my parents bought me at some tourist trap on Hollywood Boulevard, in case I really want to make sure my imaginary crewmembers can hear me from my bedroom.

I always anticipate with horror the moment when I have to sit down and watch the editor's cut. Essentially, the editor's cut consists of the footage that has been preselected as "good" by the director and placed into a coherent order by the editor, typically the order in which the scenes are arranged as written in the script. **This is called the assembly**. I'm sure most directors share this same apprehension about this moment—it is a tremendously agonizing experience for both director and editor. The editor is fully aware that he has taken your newborn baby and assumed parental responsibility over it for a period of weeks.

It is also the moment when you know if the editor "gets it," or at least gets it enough for you to allow him to not only continue looking after your child, but also to reconfigure its limbs, gender and vital organs. Or it ends up being the moment you need to find another editor.

Or you just edit the thing yourself.

In an ideal world, you've interviewed numerous editors and made your choice prior to shooting. However, independent filmmaking often does not afford this luxury, and it didn't afford it in my case. Yes, editing is done in post-production; however, as I mentioned in the last chapter, I recommend recruiting an editor while in pre-production who can be there with you on set. Along with the script supervisor, the editor can help ensure that the shots you're setting up will cut together properly. If you have dailies, he may watch them, either with you or while you are asleep, and suggest other shots that can help advance the narrative, or shots that you absolutely need to make the scene flow properly, i.e., shots you will kick yourself for not getting if someone, like an editor, doesn't speak up during production.

We were subletting editing space from our visual effects supervisor Jamison Goei at The Lot, which used to be the original Warner Brothers studio lot back in the day. It sits right across from the classic Formosa Café, where the stars would go for martinis after shooting at the studio. In the 1950s, it was Samuel Goldwyn Studios, which was home to films like *Some Like It Hot* and *West Side Story*. Frank Sinatra even had his office there. The Lot had an old Hollywood nostalgia that wafted through the air, into the buildings, and through their corridors. It was undeniable. I imagine the place hadn't changed much. There were still ashtrays in the bathroom stalls, vestigial remnants of a time when Ol' Blue Eyes and Dean Martin used to smoke cigars while they relieved themselves. I swore I could still smell the smoke. George Lucas filmed the cantina scenes from *Star Wars* there, and the soundstages were now occupied by the sets of HBO's *True Blood*.

I could not help but smile every time I stepped onto the lot and walked to my suite. This punk from Yonkers was playing ball with the big-boys! At least that's what it seemed like at the time, and it was hard to believe.

When I sat through the first screening of the editor's cut for *Detour*, my stomach was tied in knots. Fortunately, my anxieties were soon put at ease. Kirk did a great job, especially on the harrowing and climactic tunnel sequence (much of which barely changed from editor's cut to final cut). He was accustomed to editing thrillers, and that's what we set out to make, so it was clearly a good fit. It is extremely difficult to get any editor to work for peanuts, let alone a feature editor who has cut close to forty features, credited and uncredited. Some of Kirk's credited work includes: *Pulse*, *The Hills Have Eyes 2*, *Insidious* and *The Conjuring*. Since *Detour* was an indie film, Kirk was still on contract with another film as he began work on ours. It was a film directed by Mario Van Peebles, which starred 50 Cent, and Kirk was obligated to go back to work on that film if he was called to do so. He thought he was finished with the film; the cut had supposedly been locked, but of course three weeks into editing *Detour* he was called back to re-cut the film.

Sometimes You Just Have to Do It Yourself

A distributor had bought Van Peebles' film and they were requesting some editorial changes. Kirk's departure, albeit temporary, was a significant blow to our workflow. However, I didn't let this bump in the road slow us down. I started editing the movie myself. I had a decent background in editing, and was familiar with Final Cut Pro, so I put my skills to the test, picked up where Kirk left off, and became a feature editor for a number of weeks.

It's vital to never lose sight of that initial DIY mentality that compelled you to write and make the movie in the first place. You must complete the film by any means necessary, and if that means you need to stray outside your field of expertise, even if you are forced to learn on the fly, then you must do so.

I did some costume design, some production design, some prop-master work, some location scouting, I did all of the casting myself, I raised money, I drove equipment trucks on occasion (shhh, don't tell the Teamsters), I doubled my hands and arms for Neil's for most of the inserts, and I edited a portion of the film. "If you want something done, you got to do it yourself," as Jackson Alder says in *Detour*. Of course, I didn't do everything myself, not even close to it, but it is important to be willing to step in if you have to.

A BRIEF LECTURE ON FINAL CUT

You must never take your hands off the reins as leader of the project, helmer of the vision, a position that extends from the script to the screen. While in production, on the set, the status of the director is sovereign—the filmmaking hierarchy is designed to be that way. Production is a high stress pressure-cooker of an environment, so having a single individual helm the ship and keep everyone steered in the same direction is absolutely essential.

On larger studio films, I assume the director could get fired if he or she disagreed with a producer, if said producer did encroach on the director's creative territory, but it's the director's job to lose. **You have to maintain your vision, be confident in it, adapt when necessary, but always remain true to the heart of the original idea. That is your job.**

I had *final cut* of the film written into my contract. I knew most of the people investing in the film, and I acted very much in a producer capacity for years, so for me to accept anything less than final cut of the film was unacceptable. The following is the language that was used verbatim in my director's agreement:

6.1.2 Final Cut. Company and Artist shall have mutual approval of the Final Cut provided <u>the Artist's decision shall control in the event of a deadlock.</u>

I understand it is often difficult, or near impossible in some instances, for a director to retain final cut on a major motion picture. This baffles me, simply because the director is the one who is best suited to oversee the editing of his film. Filmmaking is a process that is indeed collaborative, and that collaboration is held together by the glue that is the director's vision.

If a producer steps in and re-cuts it, or a second editor is hired to re-cut it without the supervision of the director, that is *not* how it is supposed to be, unless the director is negligent in his filmmaking responsibilities and doesn't deliver what he promised.

If a film makes it all the way to an editing room, it often means someone invested many thousands, if not millions, of dollars into the vision the director posed to this financier at the start. For someone other than the director to finish it is mind-boggling, and as a consequence, such a replacement should also be disconcerting for the investor. I surmise this practice has something to do with risk-assessment, which I discussed earlier. I think there is a belief that if the production company or studio that is financially backing the film has final cut, there is less risk involved. I think this belief is misguided. There is only less risk involved if the production company or studio knows how to make a better film than the director does. And if that's the case, this begs the question: why did they hire the director to make the film in the first place?

I will now cease my digression on the subject of final cut and continue along with my regularly scheduled lesson plan.

We'll Fix It in Post

As the cutting progressed, I began meeting with Jamison about our visual effects. We talked through the shots where we were going to need to add computer-generated (CGI) effects. Jamison is supremely talented and he had this amazing idea for the final shot of the film. In the script, the final scene simply read:

```
EXT. CANYON ROAD, MUDSLIDE - SUNRISE

Hold TIGHT on an area of dried mud.

Holding. Long enough to wonder if Jackson has
died.

Then a hand PUNCHES through the ground, punc-
turing the surface, reaching up toward the sky
in the center of the frame.
```

It is to-the-point and suspenseful. We intentionally withhold the moment that he penetrates the surface of the ground just long enough for the audience to doubt Jackson's ability to escape, and then pay off the waiting with this image of physical and mental triumph.

Jamison allowed us to take this concept a step further.

Melanie at one point mentioned the idea of setting this triumphant moment against a backdrop of an even greater calamity, putting this individual's personal success in the context of a more widespread disaster that was not only affecting him, but affecting the population of the entire city, and perhaps even the entire world. I thought the idea was terrific. It had never occurred to me before because such a concept, however satisfyingly dramatic a conclusion to the story it could be, seemed completely outside the boundaries of our budget and filmmaking resources. The idea just didn't seem possible. But Jamison made it possible.

He was able to paint a background of greater Los Angeles, using a series of photographs, CGI and digital effects, so that when Jackson's hand burst through the ground, the camera would rise up, as if the force of his hand pushed the camera into the air, and tilt toward the horizon that depicted a city devastated by an earthquake, a tableau complete with smoke, fires, helicopters, spinning lights of rescue vehicles and the gigantic mudslide extending along the mountainside within which he's been trapped this whole time.

It was stunning. It was kind of like magic. I didn't bother to ask him how he was going to do it, and later how he indeed did it. I just relished what he had done and was duly impressed at how it strengthened the end of the film.

This conclusion was more or less the only visual effect we had discussed in pre-production, since a lot of the time visual effects are employed after the fact. It is often now the case that if you screw up something in production, the issue can be addressed and rectified by using visual effects. Hence the common, but despised, phrase: *Don't worry, we'll fix it in post*. It is a phrase that has become more common for directors to use, and a phrase that's become more and more despised by the VFX personnel whom these directors beg for help after they've finished shooting. Needless to say, once we realized Jamison was so deft at these black arts, we of course begged him to work his magic on close to 50 other shots.

Bless his generous heart.

TAKING THE BABY ON ITS FIRST OUTINGS

Once we arrived at a decent rough cut, we all decided to begin the test screening process. This can be a very traumatic experience for many filmmakers, since it is the first moment the film—the filmmaker's baby—is displayed in public. And this first exposure is expressly to invite criticism. It's just as horrifying as it sounds. But, like mostly anything in life, the more of these things that you suffer through, the easier they become to swallow. This is a process that is divided into chunks, and these chunks could not have been more helpful for *Detour*.

The First Screening

The first "screening" isn't really a screening, but is just as traumatic. It's when the producers say they will be "dropping by" the editing room to check out the footage.

This is early on in the post-production process, shortly after the editor's cut, and—even though the producers claim they understand that they're aware we've only just begun, that most of the scenes are barely cut together, and that we are still working on it; even though they insist that it's just an informal visit to check out what we shot because they've been dying to see something cut together since production started—it's still terrifying.

And I can't help but imagine that part of their motive includes ascertaining whether or not *we know what the heck we're doing.*

When the producers arrived, Kirk was visibly nervous, which is saying something because this guy was usually so cool and collected I'd often wonder if I should check him for a pulse. He does not eat lunch, either; he just shows up, cuts and cuts and cuts, and then leaves late in the night. I could have sworn the man was some kind of robot. Perfect disposition for a picture editor, that's for sure. After the obligatory few minutes of ice-breaking conversation, the producers assured us that they just wanted to casually check some stuff out. They were there more as excited collaborators itching to see something rather than staunch critics scrutinizing material that could either polish or tarnish their budding careers.

Kirk glanced at me, and I asked him to cue up two scenes—the very two scenes Kirk had not done *any* further work on. He kept on staring at me after I said what I said, as if continuing to look at me might elicit another, and altogether different, response. It did not. Kirk cued up the scenes, his face exhibiting a somewhat self-conscious shade of iridescent pink as he pressed Play.

It was probably incorrect to have called these excerpts scenes; they were more like randomly glued together dailies. There was a coherent logic to them, but they were excruciatingly long and extremely repetitive. Be that as it may, as much as I just wanted to fast-forward through them, I made everyone sit through each frame of them. After we finished playing both of these scenes, our producers had only complementary things to say, which was both absurd and just what I expected, and then they promptly left.

Kirk and I obviously had a lot of work to do.

The millisecond they left, Kirk turned to me with panic in his eyes: "Will, why the hell did you show them those scenes?! They're terrible. There were ones in much better shape than those you could've showed."

I looked him straight in those eyes and reassured him, "Kirk, don't worry about it, they're not gonna fire us. That's precisely why I showed them those scenes. So they'll leave us alone for a while. After watching those scenes, they couldn't possibly think we're running on schedule. They're going to have to give us more time."

In my experience with the editing process, as much as the producers push you to hurry up and finish, the director pushes back in an effort to slow it down and buy a little more time, because more time in the editing room frequently leads to more objectivity toward the film and ultimately to better results.

The more time we had to cut *Detour*, the better and better the film got, and this fact became evident in these test screenings.

The Second Screening (Actually the First Real Test Screening)

The second screening took place in the living room of our producer Diane Becker's apartment for a group of close peers in the industry, people who were smart, whose opinions meant a lot to us, and who would not have a problem being honest in their criticism. As much as I was happy that we had put together a rough cut, I was under no illusions that it was anything other than what we intended: rough. We had serious work to do and wanted our friends to help point us to the parts that needed the most attention. The running time of this version was about 105 minutes, and I had written and directed this film to be approximately 90 to 95 minutes long.

The film at this point had a number of setbacks, all of which were noticed by the folks who watched it. It had pacing problems and the character development was slow. Everyone agreed that they wanted to get to know the character of Jackson sooner. The first act consists of a man waking up in a car after an accident—he is disoriented, and every window of the car is flush with mud. In the context of the movie, he is alone until the end of the first act when he begins to use his iPhone to access videos of his girlfriend. About 25 minutes pass until we introduce his girlfriend, and in doing so, begin to flesh out Jackson's character.

It is a difficult task to deliver exposition and illustrate a backstory when there is only a single character in a single location, a location that is extremely limited with respect to space and to details that would help shed some light on his character. I'm sure the interiors of peoples' cars reflect their personality and character to a degree, but to much less of an extent than a house, for example, which is an environment filled with a lifetime of objects and personal modifications from which a viewer can extrapolate character. Without the character simply turning to the lens and offering, "Hi, I'm Jackson, if you got a few minutes, let me tell you a little bit about myself..." it's quite a challenge to explore his character with any semblance of depth this early on in the film.

Interestingly enough, I've had a great deal of experience making films that involve minimal characters in minimal locations. In my AFI thesis, *Shadowbox*, the audience is introduced to three people being held captive by a mysterious interrogator.

These people are clearly POWs; however, I never once allude to the period of time or what the specific war is. I even incorporated props of various different eras to strengthen this ambiguity: the lights that illuminate the captives as the interrogator films them are modern work lights we bought at The Home Depot, but the device through which he is filming them is a vintage Bell & Howell wind-up 16mm camera from the 1950s. Some of my classmates thought it was a mistake to not divulge the context of the time period and they demanded to know what war was taking place and what sides these people were on.

I could not have disagreed more. I argued that if the viewer were a compassionate human being, he or she would relate to the character simply as a human being who relates to another human being in a life-or-death situation. For me, the connection to the characters was a matter of biology. Here is an excerpt from the press kit for *Shadowbox*:

> The characters and location in this film are intentionally stripped of identity and historical context as a means of introducing only human beings in a torturous environment. The idea of filming or videotaping an act of violence, then using the media to distribute the images to the public, is where terrorism finds its origins. When a single act of violence is recorded and broadcast, its potency and immediacy multiplies tenfold, becoming even more powerful than, say, one hundred acts of violence that go unnoticed.
>
> The fundamental use of visual mediums as an instrument of war— as a weapon—is what differentiates this type of war from others. In *Shadowbox*, the Interrogator uses the camera as another instrument of fear and torture—the fear being rooted in the idea that others will see this torture, and that the soldiers' vulnerability and cowardice will be exposed.

With respect to the making of *Detour*, I was banking on the audience making a similar connection. I was hoping they would relate to Jackson as if he were one of them catapulted into this death-defying situation. It was a predicament that could happen to anyone, regardless of ethnicity, social class, or region of the world. If you own a car, you could get trapped in it, and if you did get trapped in it, what would you do to extricate yourself from this situation?

I wanted to tap into universal fears, and while I wanted Jackson to be a unique character, I also wanted him to be *every* character; I wanted him to be a channel through which the audience could live this story. I wanted the film to be a vicarious thrill ride.

We learn about a character through his actions, yet we empathize with the character by understanding the context in which the character takes these actions. The context in the broadest sense is where the character has been, where the character is as he takes this action, and where the character is going next. The hints we're given about the character's past, present, and future life color his actions and that subtext helps the audience understand the character's motivations, needs and desires. It allows them to see this character within the framework of their own lives and to conversely place themselves into his life.

The Third Screening (Actually the Second Real Test Screening)

The third screening took place in a much bigger living room, one with a projector and a screen and several lounge chairs lined up in rows in front of the screen. The audience consisted of approximately 25 people and we invited conversation after the screening.

Whereas the previous screening was much more casual and I knew everyone, in this screening I did not know everyone. I also decided to remove myself from the conversation altogether. The last thing the director wants to do is discourage criticism, no matter how unhelpful the director thinks the criticism is, by arguing or disagreeing with the audience members—doing so is a surefire way to clam everyone up, and then the whole exercise is pointless. I just sat back and listened, no matter how hard that was to do.

This screening, and the reaction that accompanied it, proved vital to how we revised the film on the next go-around and resulted in us cutting an entire storyline from the movie. It became very clear that a lot of people were confused by the backstory involving a miscarriage.

In the story, Jackson is a hesitant father-to-be because he and his girlfriend had previously endured a traumatic miscarriage and he is afraid that it might happen again. The way I chose to reveal this backstory was through a series of flashbacks, which were designed as puzzle pieces meant for the viewer to put together in their heads and figure out what happened. The issue that arose, however, was that some audience members did not fully understand that his girlfriend was pregnant for a second time. Some viewers thought that what was revealed was only one pregnancy, and not two. They didn't understand that a first pregnancy ended in a miscarriage, and that the girlfriend's clearly visible pregnancy was actually the second. Some thought that when Jackson leaves a video message to his baby, before he attempts to cheat death and escape, he is talking to a dead baby, the baby that was miscarried.

This did not make sense in the story, nor was it something that I wanted to imply even in the subtlest sense. If he was indeed speaking to a dead baby, how does that provide him with motivation to get out and see his baby? Emotionally, it did not make sense, and factually, it was absurd. Regardless, viewers were still coming away with that notion. Not everyone came to the same conclusion, but a large enough number for me to be genuinely concerned.

This was a significant blow for both me and Dwight, as the miscarriage played a large part in the motivations behind Jackson as we wrote him. It also played a direct role in how the actors played the scenes, what tactics they chose, what sense memory they tapped into, and what objectives they played. But that was all in the past; all that mattered was what was on the screen and how it played to an audience, and we could still manipulate it if we had to.

And manipulate it we did.

While removing the miscarriage backstory dulled the impact of Jackson's emotional arc and motivation to escape, for me at least, it did not take away from the fact that he wanted to get out of there to embrace his role as a father, and most likely his role as a future husband. Whether or not he and Laurie experienced the tragedy of a late-term miscarriage, the primal motivation to rise above his circumstances was very much there, and it was intrinsic, it was strong, and all the seeds had been planted properly. The audience was going with it, they were rooting for Jackson, whether they were privy to the original backstory or not. I was biased because I knew it, I wrote it, but its removal did not affect the story negatively in the slightest; it enhanced it.

Without the objective input from this test screening, and the reinforcement of subsequent input that was similar, I might not have made the decision to cut this storyline, and it was the right decision to do so.

The Fourth Screening (Actually the Third Real Test Screening)

The fourth screening took place at the Frankovich Barnes Screening Room on the campus of AFI. Since the last screening, we had taken out thirteen minutes of the film, clocking it in at 87 minutes. It was tight and this was going to be the last screening. This is the screening where you should get as many people as possible to attend, and especially as many people as possible who are *not* in this business. This is the screening where you want to try to gauge the reaction you might get from a random audience seeing your film in a multiplex somewhere in the middle of the country and far away from Hollywood. These circumstances are often difficult to replicate, but try to do the best you can.

There were 50 to 75 people in attendance. This time we had questionnaires that we distributed, which we kindly asked audience members to fill out and hand in after watching the film. The questionnaire that we put together consisted of the following questions:

1. Were you ever confused about what was happening?

2. How was the pacing? Did you ever feel it moved too slowly? Too fast?

3. How would you describe the tone? Was it consistent?

4. What was the scariest/most intense moment for you?

5. What did you like the best? The least?

6. Did anything take you out of the experience?

7. Can you relate to Jackson and his situation?

8. What other movies remind you of *Detour*?

9. How would you describe this movie to someone who knows nothing about it?

This was by far our most successful test screening. If you've listened to the feedback and implemented the changes that you thought enhanced and streamlined the story, then this screening *should* be the most successful screening. The majority of the criticism involved small details, a lot of nit-picky stuff that seemed like matters of personal taste, rather than wrenches in the mechanics of the film. This is always a good sign. One detail that a person loves on his questionnaire, another person hates on his questionnaire. Those types of reactions cancel each other out, and you're the one left to decide whose reaction is right.

And that is a real good place to be: finally a decision that you're allowed to make based completely on your personal preference. If you get to this point, then you certainly deserve it.

Test screenings this late in the game are most useful in discerning issues of pacing. At this point in the process, the hope is that you've been able to construct the story properly on screen, and all issues concerning confusion, clarity and plot have been left by the wayside.

Now it's an issue of *feel*. Where is it dragging? Where is it moving too fast? You are building an emotional rollercoaster ride and you must pay specific attention to the folks riding it.

At this last screening, sit near the back and watch people's reactions. You've seen the film a million times; there's no need to watch it again. Watch the audience. When are they looking away, looking bored or, God forbid, falling asleep? When are their mouths open, faces cringing, muscles tensing? When are they laughing? When are they crying?

Part of your job as a director is to observe human behavior, so make full use of that skill in this screening and bring what you observed back into the editing room with you as you tweak the final cut.

THE END IS IN SIGHT, ALMOST

As the cut approaches its locked status, there is an almost audible sigh of relief for all parties involved. Post-production is no longer as pressure-filled, but you can't let that lapse into chaos—you've got to keep that train rolling to the terminal. After our last successful screening, I continued to work on the film's score, sound design and visual effects. I also began to deal with the movie's marketing.

Finding a Title with the Perfect First Letter

During a break from the editing room, the producers and I got together to discuss the title of the film. It was currently called *Off Road* and my collaborators weren't crazy about it. I admit that I liked it a lot. In fact, I liked it better than *Buried*, which we nixed because of the Ryan Reynolds movie of the same title. I felt it had metaphorical significance. Jackson had been literally pushed off the road by a mudslide, but he had also let his personal life be pushed off its path, and he needed to transform himself to get his life back on track.

I feel that a title should be indicative of both plot and theme—the best titles are. However, there was concern that *Off Road* would misleadingly conjure images of motocross racing. I recognized the concern and thought it was valid, but the artist in me thought the title of the film should not be determined by marketing, it should be determined by story; specifically, what word or phrase is most emblematic of the story.

I told the producers that I felt there was a disturbing trend in the business that involved movies being tailored to the needs of marketing campaigns, rather than marketing campaigns being tailored to the needs of the film. **The producers had a job to do, nevertheless, and part of their job included getting the movie seen. No director on this planet doesn't want his movie to be seen.**

I was playing devil's advocate in part, but I should have been more reasonable in retrospect. As I thought more about the title, the more reasonable I became. Melanie had a great deal of experience in the Video On Demand world, and she pointed out why VOD titles beginning with a letter higher in the alphabet get greater amounts of views. It turns out that a lot of people looking for a movie at home usually scan through the first few options and then make their decision without scanning through the rest, long before they get to the film called *Off Road*.

I acquiesced to this logic and gave the title some thought. Here's the list of alternatives that I came up with, regardless of where the first letter fell in the alphabet:

Short List:

Mud Man

Rat's Rabbits (a play on the key song used in the film)

The Five Stages of Jackson Alder

Detour

Alternate Route

Extended List:

Sport Utility Vehicle

My Name is Mud

The Tomb of Jeep

Endeara Springs

The Road to Endeara Springs

Under the Surface

Baby Blue Eyes

Force Majeure

Mudslide

The Last Pitch or The Pitch

The Curve

Underneath the Pitch

Into the Pitch

The Last Will & Testament of Jackson Alder

The Bowels of the Underground

The Plunge

Once I got on this re-titling kick, I must admit that I really loved *Mud Man*. It had a primal quality to it, it had a cultish-quality to it, like *Eraserhead* or *Mad Max* had. There were horror-movie aspects to the film, which this title seemed to encompass, and it was also a reference to the advertising world and *Mad Men* (the AMC show about advertising executives who work hard and play hard on Madison Avenue). Jackson was himself an ad man, an ad man who is on his way to going quite literally mad. Nobody else shared my enthusiasm, and "M" was only two letters higher than "O."

Eventually, we agreed on *Detour*, a title that we were all excited about and saw a lot of marketing potential in if used properly. There have been other movies entitled *Detour*, but most are decades old and some long forgotten, and you can't copyright a title, so it didn't really worry me. As long as there wasn't a mudslide movie called *Detour*, I felt like we were in the clear.

Adding a Score

Henning Lohner was busy working on the score. However, he was working on the score in Berlin, Germany. I was familiar with Henning's previous work and was confident that his style was perfect for the film, so I felt very secure in his ability to work on the music from so far away.

Typically, I am extremely involved with the score of my films. I am a musician myself and believe, in many ways, that sound is 51% of a film. It can make or break a movie. Therefore to not be able to work alongside Henning was a first for me in the post-production process and it was disconcerting.

I also reached out to my friend Leon Dewan, who lent us some of his wonderful Dewanatron tones for the film. Leon and his cousin, Brian Dewan, build handmade analog synthesizers and are famous for their "Swarmatron," which Trent Reznor used to score his Oscar-Winning soundtrack for *The Social Network*. Dewanatron produces the best droning sounds in the business, in my opinion. Henning was very open to having Leon contribute to the score and it also reassured me to have someone in the United States working on the film's soundscape.

Henning, as it turned out, was a consummate professional and he churned out quality music. We only had three revisions of the score, revisions that involved Henning addressing my notes and then rescoring. Even though we were a great distance apart, he knew exactly what I wanted, exactly what I was going for, despite the fact that it's often extremely difficult to articulate thoughts and feelings regarding music. What he was also able to do, which for some composers may have been impossible, was take Leon's unique Dewanatron tones and beats that I had specifically referenced and liked, and integrate them into his own compositions. He was able to alter the key and rhythm and seamlessly merge the material into his own music. I had asked Henning to do this, half-expecting him to be offended by such a request, but he took it as a challenge and his composition thrived as a result.

No matter how hesitant you may be about voicing your opinion, you must do it even if you think someone may not want to hear it. The film comes first, and if something is not sounding right, or you think that something might sound better with a particular adjustment, you go ahead and let all the relevant collaborators know.

You are the director; your opinion *is* the vision of the film. There will always be moments when you wish someone else would say something on your behalf, or you would rather not mention it at all and see if the problem fixes itself. These are not solutions. Remember, while the director is often the one praised for the success of a film, he or she is also the one saddled with the tremendous and unenviable responsibility if the film fails.

Henning was part of the Hans Zimmer school of movie scoring, which I soon found out had forever altered the notion of the "original score." With the advent of digital archiving, and more and more composers retaining the rights to their movie compositions, the practice of reusing scores from previous films has become more prevalent. I had no idea this was so common, let alone so accepted by filmmakers.

Henning had planned to use some material for *Detour* that he had used in a previous movie of his. Some filmmakers may not have minded this. One might even argue that the filmmaker is getting a bigger bang for his buck (i.e., Joe "Indie" Filmmaker can't afford to hire an orchestra to perform the composer's score, but he can use bits and pieces from the multi-million dollar picture the composer was hired to score a few years ago). I personally feel that every aspect of a film should be as unique as the vision itself. I mention this only because I was completely unaware that many modern composers now utilize material from their archives to build the score for new films.

Once I mentioned to Henning that I wanted to build as much of the score from scratch as possible, he was completely fine with it— it wasn't even close to being a problem. I want to make sure you are mindful of this modern shift in the scoring business when you begin to talk through the score with your composer. It is important to maintain a level of transparency in your communications with all creative departments.

In many respects, the mark of a good director is if your collaborators want to work with you again. If your film is good, that helps as well. A leader will always invite resentment, in whichever industry or political realm he rules, but ultimately it's your choice—you don't have to direct movies, now do you?

The Sound of Incompetence

The sound process in post-production is an important business. As I just said, sound and music can make or break a film, and it is the final phase. You have spent years getting your film into the shape it is in, and then suddenly so close to the finish line, there is no money left, or there is very little money left, and you need to ensure that the film sounds good. It is very tempting to skimp on this part of the process, but I can tell you from personal experience, please don't make the same mistake I did.

Detour was a particularly challenging movie to design sound for. If you divide the film into its two basic elements of protagonist and antagonist, it comes down to *man vs. mud*. Since the narrative is told through Jackson's POV, we see his enemy the way he does: through the windows. Until the mud actually begins to physically invade the car, it is principally an invisible antagonist. Therefore, sound was to play a critical role in conveying the "threat" of this antagonist, an antagonist that no one watching the first half of the film can actually see.

Even when you finally do see it, you're not visually aware of how much mud there is, beyond the mud you're seeing on screen. You guess there's probably a lot—it's a mudslide, and nature is a heartless bitch—but you're not being given that information visually. Ethan Friedericks, our primary sound designer, and I came up with an idea called the "Mud Monster" that would act as a sound motif through-out the film.

Much like the recurring score in *Jaws* that telegraphed the appearances of the lethal Great White Shark, the Mud Monster— a mixture of crunching, cracking, creaking and ominous dread— would foreshadow the devastation that was threatened by our film's antagonist.

This was just one example of what made the post-sound on *Detour* challenging, and what made finding a sound house that could fulfill our creative needs within our miniscule budget even more challeng-ing. We were finally seduced by the promise of a $100,000 sound mix for $10,000, which was made to us by a particular sound house. You know something is too good to be true when it actually seems too good to be true. However, our guard was down. We had such great experiences with our other collaborators in post, all of whom were working for peanuts, we went ahead and believed the bill of goods that was sold to us and signed with this house.

Not only was their sound work subpar, but they also had not com-pleted the dialogue editing before we hit the mixing stage. This was an egregious oversight and something any legitimate sound house would scoff at.

When a film hits the mixing stage, everything must be ready to go, including: sound editing, dialogue editing, sound design, sound effects, score, source music, Foley and ADR (Additional Dialogue Recording). All of these elements must be completed, processed and ready for implementation when the mix begins. Rent-ing a proper mixing stage, something that closely resembles the size and feel of a genuine movie theater (that is the target venue you're mixing the sound for) is quite costly, so it is imperative that your sound house has crossed its t's and dotted its i's before they commence this process.

Basically, dialogue editing consists of a sound editor sifting through the film's audio tracks, cutting out the noise and unnecessary parts, and cleaning the sound of the dialogue. I cannot stress how crucial it is to properly complete your dialogue editing prior to the mix, especially on a low-budget film.

In the latter half of *Detour* there is a lot of action, and I directed much of the action verbally during the takes. The director's voice on the dialogue tracks is the bane of any dialogue editor's workday, but it is part of the craft and therefore comes with the territory. The dialogue editor should have gone in and cut out all the instances when I gave direction to Neil during the takes, in addition to cleaning up and cutting out excess production noise and the like. But he did not. In fact, the dialogue track for each reel had not even been touched. They did not even go to any lengths to hide this: one look at the Pro Tools session on the mixing stage and I could plainly see the track had not been touched. If proper dialogue editing had indeed occurred, the track would be cut to pieces and marked up and blocks of ADR would be above and/or below the track.

Clearly, we must have seemed like bumpkins right off the bus to them, because it was painfully obvious that we were being taken advantage of. They attempted to cut the dialogue right there on the stage, and in doing so, knock us horrendously behind schedule—until we eventually caught onto their shenanigans and exposed them as the frauds that they were. It is difficult to hide the fact that your workflow has slowed to a quarter of its intended speed.

Unfortunately, we had already paid them 90% of their fee up front. This was our mistake, but we've since learned from it. So we finished out the scheduled mixing session, which was primarily spent finishing the dialogue editing that they were contracted and obligated to do weeks prior, and then promptly fired them. We ended up hiring Monkeyland Audio in Burbank to help fix the film and finish our sound, and they did a tremendous job. They quite literally saved the sound.

Become familiar with all the services required from a proper sound house, because there are plenty of people and companies out

there waiting to take advantage of student filmmakers and independent filmmakers. Post-sound is a part of the filmmaking process that most first-time filmmakers are often less familiar with than other aspects of the process, and predators are acutely aware of this. Most film schools do not teach sound design to their fellows; this is an aspect of the process that is frequently learned on the job.

Do your research, get recommendations, and make sure they deliver what they promise to deliver.

SUMMARY

In post-production, the film that you'd conceived and nurtured now goes into the world, where it is judged by strangers who may not love it as much as you do. But that's a good thing, because it often takes an objective eye to see the problems that you might be willfully blind to. This is the time where your initial vision may be forced to change, and if you are open to useful criticism, it can change for the better. Remember, though, that you are still the director. Even though you collaborate with others, you're the one who ultimately makes the decisions that will shape the final film.

DISTRIBUTION

As we approached the bittersweet end of the filmmaking process for *Detour*, what often happens to independent films happened to us: we ran out of money. Luckily, however, we did have a copy of the locked final cut, albeit with temporary sound design and without color correction.

FINDING FINISHING FUNDS

It is much easier to find finishing funds when you actually have something to show investors, rather than the reverse, when you're trying to get development money for what is merely an idea, or at most, a script. That's the hardest sell there is.

We showed the unfinished film to a few contacts in the industry and were immediately overwhelmed with positive reactions, mostly from a company called Level 1 Entertainment, which had produced films like *Rendition*, *Strange Wilderness*, and *Grandma's Boy*. We screened the film for the president of the company, Bill Todman, Jr., who was completely engrossed throughout the viewing. When the film finished and the lights went up, Bill turned to me and said, "How much to buy the film?" We roughly knew how much we needed to finish the film and pay back investors, and named our number, to which he replied: "That's the price of a first draft...who do I write the check to?"

This was the best meeting I ever had, hands down. We suddenly had finishing funds and a major production company behind us. The endorphins were rushing to my brain that day.

What Level 1 saw in *Detour* was the thrust of an emotional character film fashioned into a marketable genre: a disaster-thriller. It was also a film made on a shoestring budget that looked much more expensive to make than it actually was. **The benefit of staging an entire film more or less in a single location is that you can devote all of your resources to the production value of that single location.** Your focus is sharpened; it is funneled into one single direction. Having each one of your collaborators focused in the same direction, while confronting the obvious limitations inherent in such an endeavor, fosters creativity in the most unadulterated of senses. There is no multi-tasking or side-projects, there's one single goal.

In this age of microbudget filmmaking, do not attempt to produce a larger script on a smaller budget. You must now write with a budget in mind. This is diametrically opposed to what I was taught in school—never let budget dictate your creative vision on the page. We now live in a new era of economical filmmaking, and do you want to make a movie or not?

As terrific as this deal sounded, it did not come to fruition nearly as easily as I thought it would. Since Level 1 had never dealt in the business of independent filmmaking before, nor had they ever bought a finished (well, semi-finished) product, the deal did stall the momentum for quite a while.

In order to free up the money necessary to pay the vendors we owed, and pay our new sound house to finish the mix, we needed to complete a lengthy contract process. In one respect, you may sideline a lot of paperwork by just making the movie yourself; however, once you try to then take that finished film and integrate it into the system that you were making it outside of, it becomes an exercise in red-tape, legalese and paper cuts to the brain. We had to wait over a year, longer than it took to take the movie from production through the final cut of the edit, before we were able to sign the contracts and finish post-production. In fact, much of the time we were waiting on original investors to sign off on the new deal since they had to be bought out of the film. And they had lawyers too, who had to deal with our lawyers, who then had to deal with Level 1's lawyers. It was a Sisyphean ordeal that could try the patience of most Tibetan monks.

The irony was that, while we began this project because we were sick and tired of waiting for Hollywood, we were now waiting for Hollywood to buy it. It's sick and twisted, the whole business.

FINDING DISTRIBUTION—
AND, NO, IT'S NOT THE SAME AS *BURIED*

Level 1 hired a producer's representative, which as far as I can tell is the same thing as a sale's rep: a liaison to the film who pitches the film to distributors. These are the same people who flock to film festivals to acquire films. When our rep took the film around to various distributors, most of the initial feedback was disappointing, to say the least.

Their responses made it crystal clear that these distributors only cared about two things:

1. It sounds like *Buried*.

2. Who is Neil Hopkins?

Honestly, I almost think some of these distributors did not watch the film. There was a shared reticence that involved the challenge of marketing a film that, upon first glance, sounded similar to *Buried*, and that starred someone who was not nearly as famous as, say, Ryan Reynolds. The responses from those who did watch the film were mostly terrific. Everyone seemed to like it. However, the two points above still plagued their perception of the film. Remember, I wrote this script in 2008, before *Buried*, before *127 Hours*, before *Frozen*, before *Brake*, before *Wrecked*, before *Gravity*, before *All Is Lost*, before the apparent trend for this type of minimalist action film. These gave the distributors pause, and understandably so.

However, there are multiple stories to be told within any genre, and despite sharing a minimalist survival theme, these other films are dealing with very different protagonists in very different circumstances.

Vive la Différence!

I subscribe to the notion that a dramatic character is defined by his or her behavior; specifically, his or her proactive attempts to rise above the given circumstances. However, if the circumstances are too dire and too limiting, the character has nowhere to go, nothing to do to help himself, and the end is inevitable. While Jackson Alder is stuck in a confined environment in *Detour*, he is stuck in an SUV. None of his body parts are ensnared and the size of his car, when compared to a coffin, looks more like the interior of the Taj Mahal. Jackson is free to move around his environment; he can investigate his situation and utilize the abundant tools around him in order to try and escape (tools that most of us have in our own cars: a bottle of water, "The Club," camping chairs—tools that we never thought in a million years we would need to get us out of such a horrible situation).

The intention of the film is for it to be a story where the audience can picture themselves in their own car, in this same exact situation and ask: *What would I do to survive? Would I do what he's doing? Oh, that's a good idea...or, no that's a terrible idea, don't do that!* The audience needs to relate to the main character, needs to be able to put themselves into his shoes. I wanted Jackson to be an "everyman."

Buried, on the other hand, depicts a situation that most anyone would find horrifying. The character is an American contractor living in Iraq who is kidnapped by terrorists. This is a job that is as foreign to most Americans as Iraq is, an occupation that carries with it risks and pressures that most regular people never encounter. The main character in *127 Hours* is an adventurer. I like to go for hikes every once in a while, but this guy, Aaron Ralston, left his job with Intel in order to pursue a life of climbing mountains. Ralston is a real person, and the movie is based on a true story, but his on-the-edge existence is far too daring for most of us to embrace in our everyday lives.

Jackson Alder is both you and me. He is on his way to work and a disaster befalls him. This very same thing can happen to you, and it just might; mudslides are a common occurrence where I live in California, and I own a car. Who's to say I won't find myself in his situation?

What I can say for sure is that I would never find myself in the situation the character in *Buried* finds himself in, or the situation the character in *127 Hours* finds himself in. For me, as a director, I wanted to focus on a story that would, literally, hit home for everyone watching it.

That was the pitch, and I was hoping a distributor would swing at it.

Story and Concept Trump Stars

In a culture where a high concept increasingly trumps a well-crafted story, the onus is on the artist to reinforce the notion that story is all that really matters, story is what makes movies authentic, and story is what makes people buy a ticket at the window. Level 1 Entertainment got behind this "radical" idea, which was a great first step; however, it was not until later that Gravitas Ventures, a newcomer to the world of distribution, also got behind the film. They recognized the marketability of this specific concept and admired the execution, despite any potential concern about *Buried* or the other movies having already been released.

When Gravitas took us on, they had been building up a fantastic track record of licensing their films to Warner Brothers under their digital distribution umbrella. They had recently licensed a film to WB that was a minimalist thriller, where the concept alone had made it a success. It had no stars, but it was making a lot of money in Video On Demand. Gravitas felt confident that they could pitch *Detour* to Warner Brothers as the next film to fit within that specific successful VOD model.

Of course, I really liked the idea of WB getting involved, but it meant waiting another 4 to 6 months. It had to be pitched at just the right time. We trusted Gravitas and their instincts, and sure enough, Warner Brothers licensed the film.

HOW VOD HAS MADE A DIFFERENCE

We instantly had a reach into over 100 million homes through a digital platform. And, to top that off, we were going to get a theatrical release. The wonderful trend for independent filmmakers in today's Video On Demand market is that most digital distributors prefer a theatrical release, even if the release does not make money at the box office. The dream of every independent filmmaker is to see their film on the big screen, and in today's climate of digital distribution, that is not only an option, but a preferred option.

The reason?

If a movie is released in theaters, it not only adds to the prestige of the film—ostensibly, making it more desirable to watch—but it also allows the various Video On Demand platforms to charge an "In Theaters Now" price point to their rental fee for the first 60 days of the release. If a film bypasses the theater and goes straight to VOD, platforms can only charge regular prices, whereas, if it's in theaters, even for just a week, they can charge an extra 2 to 3 dollars per rental for 60 days.

VOD is where the distributors of independent films make their money these days, and by having a movie open in a theater as well, the potential to make an even greater amount of money increases exponentially.

It was a few years ago that only two viable options for distributing movies existed: a release to theaters or straight-to-DVD. In recent years, a third option opened up: so-called "multiplatform" releases, such as "Day & Date" and "Ultra-VOD," which allow viewers to rent or buy films on demand in the comfort of their homes around the same time the film is released in theaters. The strategy requires less promotion and marketing expense from distributors and the model can often be more profitable. While theater owners initially resisted the concept of these releases, for obvious reasons, the strategy has become commonplace following the success of films like the financial thriller *Margin Call* and the raunchy comedy *Bachelorette*.

THE REVIEWS ARE IN!

Detour opened in limited theaters nationwide, including New York and Los Angeles, and was also released in Canada. The reviews were largely positive. *The Village Voice* called the filmmaking and performance "invigorating." *The Hollywood Reporter* said it was a "thriller that fully succeeds." *The New York Times* said it was nothing short of "authentic" and a "respectable debut" for me.

A month before the release, after our PR campaign had launched to reviewers, I got tagged in a tweet by Tom Charity, the movie critic for CNN. Tom tweeted that *Detour* was the best film he had seen in 2013. I will grant you that 2013 was pretty young at that point, but it was still amazing, especially when it was coming from a critic who is notoriously tough.

Distribution vs. Publicity

The film premiered at the Chinese Theatre in Los Angeles, which was a genuine thrill. It is the theater you dream to have your film premiered at. It also ran in New York City at Cinema Village. The opening night in Manhattan was oversold to such an extent that my writing partner Dwight, who lives in New York, was unable to get in. He was supposed to do the Q&A! Our theater booker had to call the theater to rectify the problem, and after the tongue-lashing he presumably gave the manager, the staff kicked the people out of their larger theater, where a movie was already in progress, and put the *Detour* audience in there.

Dwight did get into the screening, and the Q&A did end up happening...but it almost didn't!

We had a terrific public relations company handle the rollout of our film: Prodigy PR. I can't recommend them enough. They're not cheap, but they're worth it. **The interesting thing I learned during this process is, at this level of independent film, the distributor doesn't pay for the PR, the production company does.** I, along with many others, was under the impression that once a film has distribution, the costs to the producers come to an end, more or less; that it is up to the distributor to promote the movie. This is often *not* the case, amazingly so.

Even though we had a big name like Warner Brothers behind us, who was distributing the film through its digital VOD platforms, we still had to pay for our own PR or convince someone else to do it. Once again, I had to resort to doing it myself. This time, though, I had Level 1 Entertainment behind me. They ended up funding the PR and the campaign was terrific.

Do It Yourself Distribution

There is a growing trend for the filmmakers themselves to be involved in the distribution process. This is simultaneously discouraging and encouraging because it means filmmakers no longer rely on the distribution methods of major studios. It can be discouraging if you're not offered such a distribution deal; however, the encouraging part is that filmmakers now have the ability to release movies themselves. And I'm not talking about buying a print and driving it from an art house theater in one state to another halfway across the country. I'm talking about Video On Demand: the high definition transfer of a file from your master directly to millions of homes worldwide.

Quite literally, the service that Warner Brothers provided to us is now available to anyone with a film, and at a profit percentage weighed heavily in the favor of the filmmaker.

My second feature film, *The Mirror*, is a metafictional satire about a lifestreamer obsessed with recreating scenes from movies and streaming them online. We released it in 1080p High Definition through Vimeo On Demand, a streaming service that is available in close to 100 million homes worldwide. Additionally, we—the filmmakers—make 90% of the profit, with the other 10% going to Vimeo for providing the service. It is a bold, and potentially game-changing, tool for the indie filmmaker who tends to work "outside" of the system.

If the filmmakers are in charge of promotion—whether that means marketing the film yourself or hiring a public relations company to take the promotional reigns—why let a traditional distributor profit from your hard work when you can distribute the film yourself and recoup the profits directly?

This is an important question to ask yourself if you're planning on making a microbudget film that you are raising the money for yourself. DIY has never been easier, or more professional looking, as it is right now.

THE END OF BLOCKBUSTERS?

Steven Spielberg and George Lucas recently predicted the collapse of the blockbuster. Spielberg said, "There's eventually going to be a big meltdown. There's going to be an implosion where three or four or maybe even a half dozen of these mega-budgeted movies go crashing into the ground and that's going to change the paradigm again."

There have been predictions like this before and there have been summers of mega-flops before, but I think it says something when the very creators of the blockbuster are warning us of its imminent demise. There was a time when lines of people would wrap around a city block for a movie that would stay in the theaters for not days, not weeks, but months—several months even. Today, a hit movie is lucky to live more than two or three weeks on the screen of a first-run theater.

The studios are desperate for franchises. That is their modus operandi and it seems to be their primary business model. The days when studios bankrolled unique, niche market, character-driven movies are, much to the chagrin of most adults I know, more or less over.

This is a frightening reality, especially for an indie film-lover like me who came of age in the early 90s and wanted to become a filmmaker because he saw *Pulp Fiction* on the big screen and wore out his VHS copies of the *Twin Peaks* episodes David Lynch directed. There was a respect for the art of original storytelling, with particular focus on the role of the director, in the Nineties that seems to have been in steady decline for years.

I'm not Steven Spielberg, nor am I George Lucas. I'm not a mogul. I'm the anti-mogul (this is not of my choosing, in case you're wondering) and thus I feel perfectly capable of responding to the above-referenced moguls with respect to their prediction and how it affects the world of independent cinema. There is no need for studios to fund indie films when filmmakers are taking it upon themselves to raise money and shoot their own films. I have no idea how many independent, truly independent, films get made per year, but the number has to be astonishingly high. (Figure there are about 300 major theatrical releases in most years; there must be at least ten times as many independent features produced.) The technological resources at the disposal of hungry young filmmakers these days are overwhelming, and strikingly affordable.

But here's the rub: even with access to this kind of technology, movies still cost money to make. Not as much money to make an indie film, but it still takes money...at least a little bit of it.

With a deluge of entertainers vying for an audience's attention, originality becomes the differentiator. What makes a studio think that audiences want to watch variations of the same type of movie over and over again? Okay, the stuff is a bit more polished now, younger and ostensibly hipper, popular actors have roles in the films, and the special effects are killer. But still, if this current generation is the generation that is defined by getting bored easily, that enjoys seven-second Vine videos for their amusement, why would a savvy executive think that the reboot of a movie everyone has seen, or the upteenth sequel in a franchise, is going to attract a broad audience, to say nothing of actually catching their attention? There is a clear disparity in logic, and that disparity is beginning to reflect itself in box office numbers—as predicted by Spielberg and Lucas.

The trouble with the studio system is that they're making fewer movies and putting much more money into them. They're taking huge gambles financially, so the way to offset that gamble is to ensure that the entertainment they're selling appeals to as many people as possible. This approach, of course, dilutes the originality of the content. When movies are made in boardrooms on the basis of demographics, or the desire to sell in China or other countries that buy American movies, they alienate that portion of the audience that wants to see unique, personal films. In other words, they alienate the actual film fans. Instead of making ten films that target different, more niche markets, they make one movie for the price of ten and bet it all.

As George Lucas said, "they're going for the gold." I'm no businessman, but that doesn't sound like the best business plan to me. It sounds like a recipe for losing the people most dedicated to my product.

This business model leaves zero room for experimentation or artistic risks. As a filmmaker, I find that stifling. **There must be a balance between art and commerce. If the commerce outweighs the art, then the product is doomed from the start. Emotion isn't cookie cutter, yet writers, directors and actors in this business are asked to translate emotion from the screen into the minds and hearts of viewers.** This is why independent film is so important to the art of cinema; it is why it thrived in the Nineties, because the studios were behind these types of films.

The Microbudget Revolution

My film, *The Mirror*, is partly a reaction against the Hollywood system and partly an homage to it. It is very much the opposite of the Hollywood tent-pole: it is a film that filmmakers can go out and make themselves if they have the desire to do so.

I intentionally shot the film on consumer devices like the iPhone, the GoPro, the Canon 7D, and a variety of laptop cameras. I wanted it to aesthetically replicate how a movie might look if the majority of people out there set out to make a movie. It's rough around the edges, it's handmade, but as a result, it's relevant to the way people currently see the world. They see the world through their computers, through their iPhones, through their iPads. Have you been to a concert recently? More spectators watch the concert through the filter of an iPhone or iPad, recording video, than are watching the actual live concert with their own two eyes. Isn't that strange? At this pace (and we might actually be there now), the slick, polished fare that is produced from Hollywood will become less and less familiar to the way we perceive filmed entertainment. It is becoming foreign, antiquated, and therefore less relevant.

Just like the silents before the talkies, classical actors before method actors, black and white before color, the palette upon which visual information is being mixed, matched and applied is changing. The consumer has adapted. And so must the studios.

With the exception of one scene in *The Mirror*, we limited ourselves to shooting and recording sound on devices that just about anyone can get his or her hands on. When I was a kid, I would take my grandfather's camcorder, gather my friends and go out and shoot a movie. It was exactly the same type of thing Spielberg did with his Super 8 camera when he was a kid. With *The Mirror*, I wanted to tap into that childhood idealism; I wanted the film to feel like, yeah, I love making movies, so let's go out and make one. That's why filmmakers get into the business, to make magic. However, it's often the case that the magic gets lost when the business aspect moves to the forefront of the filmmaking process.

While some of these developments in the industry are clearly discouraging to those of us who love making movies, I strongly feel that we are at the beginning of another revolution in film, a micro-budget revolution.

It took five years to make *Detour,* and during that time, I made *The Mirror.* It is a movie within a movie. A movie I made while making another movie. And within that movie are many other movies, because that is the nature of reflection. Today, reflection is becoming more and more our everyday reality: we're watching our lives through a lens, through a small screen that posts our lives onto other screens.

What is more real? That which happens before our very own eyes or something that happens on a screen. Is there really a difference anymore? This is what microbudgets are beginning to pick up on, and it is something that old school Hollywood is not taking into account.

Filmmakers are no longer the handful of A-Listers the studios hire to direct their ten tent-pole movies every summer. We are all filmmakers now. We can all make, and release, a movie.

What are you waiting for?

EPILOGUE

The one thing that I've learned, and learned to love and embrace after spending a total of five years making *Detour*, is patience.

This is an extremely stressful business, but it does not have to be as stressful as you might think. The majority of stress is undoubtedly generated from self-imposed standards, standards that I can attest to setting in my own mind, that are begged to be set because of the overwhelming rejection and lack of validation in this industry. Like many others, I have been brought up in an environment where hard work is rewarded, acknowledged, and is a stepping stone to a higher platform, a platform that's ideally one hop closer to an overarching goal. It took me a long time to make *Detour*, but during that time I was able to make another movie, *The Mirror*, and on the strength of *Detour* I was hired to make my third feature film for a major production company.

Each step leads to another; it's important to remember that progressing in this business is much more like a marathon than it is a sprint.

If you're seeking validation, Hollywood is not a place where you will find it—not usually. It's extremely important to find satisfaction and fulfillment in the *doing*, in the process of writing the script, shooting the movie, editing the film, and the like. Throughout his career, Woody Allen has been very vocal about the fact that he never watches his films once they're complete; that his role in them, and the satisfaction he's taken out of the process, is over. He releases his films to the world and then moves on to the next.

This type of mindset borders on the philosophical, but I think it's wise to take a tip from actors and their methods: live in the moment. No matter what an actor's specific technique involves, it has one thing in common with every other actor's technique. One must listen and react, and not think about what the next line is, because to think about the next line is to be inauthentic, to not be *in the moment*. This rubric can be applied to filmmaking.

Enjoy the process. Work hard, but don't work to please the future generations who might be judging you after you've left this earth. Write what you're passionate about now, be honest with your actors, live the story through them, share in their vulnerability, and direct the film in such a way that it strikes your viewers' most immediate emotional chords.

Life is short, and so are audiences' attention spans. Try to keep your film to under 95 minutes or less.

THE REALITY OF THE HOLLYWOOD DREAM

I've become inextricably tied to Hollywood, for better or worse. Living in it is like living in a college dorm masked as a municipality, replete with the drunken mishaps and plagiarized homework.

Hollywood is still very much considered The City of Dreams, and for those people who just purchased their first copy of Final Draft screenwriting software, the notion of the *spec script* is still the equivalent to a modern day gold rush. People move to the West Coast every day in pursuit of that lucrative windfall: the result of that one agent or producer reading your script at just the right time and in just the right mood, which leads to millions of dollars, your characters inhabited by A-list actors, and the second principal credit on a feature-film crawl. The allure of Hollywood, regardless of the wounded economy and widespread unemployment, is as strong as it's ever been.

Hollywood sells itself; it always has, and always will.

Take for example the HBO series, *Entourage*. The show started out a satire. Rewatch the first season; its humor is significantly broader than the subsequent seasons. The public is enamored with Hollywood, no matter how absurd or unrealistic the circumstances are that surround it. *Entourage* was meant to be a parody, in my opinion, but then viewers began to take it seriously, desiring these people's lives, lives that are completely artificial.

Sophia Coppola's film, *Somewhere*, is a fine contrast to *Entourage*. It's very much the anti-*Entourage* in the sense that it portrays the inherent emptiness in these same characters' lives, an emptiness *Entourage* leaves out to satiate the almost unquenchable appetite for the myth of Hollywood and its celebrities' lives. Who would think living in the Chateau Marmont surrounded by bare breasts would be boring, but alas, there are other things in life to strive for, to crave, to fill ourselves with. Celebrity is not an end in and of itself. It's a by-product, and it's often a by-product in the sense that it's an unwanted side effect to fame, a drug that can be harmful to you if not taken in the prescribed dose.

It's important to wade through the hype and focus on what brings you to Hollywood. It's not the fame and money that it can potentially lead to, but rather it's the battleground upon which you are given an opportunity to practice your craft, begin your career, and make your movies.

The filmmakers I admire are artists, and artists in the classical sense. This is a business, but it's an art too—it's primarily an art. And it's the job of the filmmaker to promote this ideal vigorously while working in the business. It's easy for those pulling the strings and bankrolling the movies to forget about the art or make it secondary, but the filmmaker must never let them forget about it. It's the quality of the filmmaker's vision that attracts and holds an audience, not a poster.

Filmmakers have styles that are often reflections of themselves, their personalities. Scorsese: hyper, fast-talking, his personality oozes from his recurring whip-pans, ramped push-ins and jump cuts. Kubrick: cold, detached, reclusive. Lynch: quirky, a "boy scout" with an unsettling darkness lurking just below the surface. Terrence Malick is more like a modern day Monet, stitching together the Impressionist manifestations of his characters' lives. He connects bits and pieces of moments, which are woven together through feeling, the entire meaning of which cannot fully be appreciated until the viewer takes a step back and considers all of his brushstrokes together at once from afar. His films are only linear in the sense that they start at a certain point in time and end at a later point in time, but that's not how you experience them.

Every story has been told before, but what's new is how you see a specific story through your eyes. That's the unique part—and the part you must strive to grasp hold of as you make your movie.

There is an inherent disparity between language and intent, articulation and emotion, and I found that the visual arts were a much more direct route to communication in my life. For me, personally, I find cinema to be the most direct form of communication. There are arguments to be made for the authenticity (emotionally and intellectually) of various art forms like photography, literature, painting, theatre and the performance arts; I've just been thunderstruck by this one.

Cinema resonates with me. Cinema combines all art forms to wondrous and magical effect. Cinema is my drug of choice.

Just as it takes years to learn a language beyond the basics, I propose that a dedication of a similar magnitude is necessary to learn the language of film. You can't just become a screenwriter because you know how to write an essay; it is a bit more oranges than apples. This is a craft that is learnt, practiced and suffered over, a form in which precedents have been set and yet continues to evolve. The art of cinema will be debated, discussed, analyzed and revised for years to come.

Filmmaking is an acquired skill, a language that transcends cultures oceans apart, that is taught both in the classroom and experienced in the field—and it should be respected as such.

BUT WHAT REALLY IS "REAL"?

The game has changed. It has changed exponentially. The difference between fact and fiction, and vice versa, has been shrunk to an infinitesimal degree. We now live in a world where virtually every person on the planet has a high-definition video camera built directly into his or her cell phone—and we're all filming each other with them. We're constantly filming and being filmed and we are aware that we're being filmed.

Even if we were to film "reality," the moment we film it we've taken a point of view—we've eliminated its objectivity and replaced it with the subjectivity of our camera. The lens, no matter how unscripted the material, changes everything in front of it.

As storytellers, we are searching for the truth—searching for the truth in a modern world, the truth inside ourselves. As I write this sentence, I stare at a small camera built into my computer. I've rarely used it, but perhaps someone out there is, watching me, monitoring me, keeping tabs. We inhabit a world that isn't really ours anymore; it's everyone else's. Maybe that's a good thing, maybe it will keep us on our toes, and maybe it's what will keep us honest. It certainly allows filmmakers much greater access to the tools they need to make a movie. It can be argued that there is no such thing as privacy anymore; absolutely everything is being filmed. This development only highlights the importance of teaching, and learning, the language of film.

While the medium is changing, it is our responsibility as filmmakers to remain honest and sincere in our storytelling and to the art form itself.

I'm a storyteller telling my story. I've attempted to remain uncensored, and I believe I have. I've tried hard to ride the rails of veracity, and I hope my words are of some help to you. I hope they inspire, I hope they teach, I hope they elicit a laugh, be it while reading this in Starbucks or in the lobby of CAA or in your parents' basement.

In the end, our purpose as filmmakers is akin to the purpose of the railroad, an apt metaphor that never ceases to disappoint in times of crisscrossing articulations: we are just human beings trying to connect. And it is *story* that connects us.

ABOUT THE AUTHOR

WILLIAM DICKERSON graduated from The College of The Holy Cross with a Bachelor's Degree in English and received his Master of Fine Arts in Directing from The American Film Institute. His debut feature film *Detour*, which he wrote and directed, was released through Gravitas Ventures and Warner Brothers Digital Distribution and hailed as an "Underground Hit" by *The Village Voice*, an "emotional and psychological roller-coaster ride" by *The Examiner*, and nothing short of "authentic" by *The New York Times*. He self-released his metafictional satire, *The Mirror*, which opened YoFi Fest's inaugural film festival in 2013. He recently completed his third feature film, *Don't Look Back*, for MarVista Entertainment.

His award-winning work has been recognized by film festivals across the country. His AFI Thesis Film, *Shadowbox*, won Best Short at the Shockfest Film Festival in Hollywood in 2008, and his scripts have been optioned and developed by major production companies. He has written and directed commercial content for Fox Atomic, Walden Media, Mob Scene Productions and Little, Brown and Company.

His first book, *No Alternative*, was declared, "a sympathetic coming-of-age story deeply embedded in '90s music" by Kirkus Reviews. He currently serves on AFI's Alumni Executive Board and is a Faculty Member at the New York Film Academy. He lives in Los Angeles, California.

For more information about William's films,
books, and upcoming projects, check out his website:
www.williamdickersonfilmmaker.com

CPSIA information can be obtained at www.ICGtesting.com
Printed in the USA
LVOW12s1838080615

441637LV00001B/119/P